The Varieties of Leadership at Novarum Pharmaceuticals

A Novel

The Varieties of Leadership at Novarum Pharmaceuticals

A Novel

Robert Pernick, PhD
Johns Hopkins University

Floyd Kemske
Novelist

IAP

INFORMATION AGE PUBLISHING, INC.
Charlotte, NC • www.infoagepub.com

Library of Congress Cataloging-in-Publication Data

Pernick, Robert.
The varieties of leadership at Novarum Pharmaceuticals : a novel / Robert Pernick.
p. cm.
Includes bibliographical references.
ISBN 978-1-60752-223-2 (pbk.) – ISBN 978-1-60752-224-9 (hardcover)
1. Leadership. 2. Organizational behavior. 3. Pharmaceutical industry–Management. I. Title.
HD57.7.P465 2009
658.4'092–dc22

2009025615

Printed in the United States of America

Contents

Preface

Storytelling is a time-honored way of educating, especially for students who are in the early stages of their careers. This idea is captured nicely by the following three authors:

> "Through literature dealing with organizations we can extend the range of our knowledge . . . vicarious experience can substitute for personal experience."[1]

> "Our time is as muddled as . . . [Joseph] Conrad's. The world of planning and crystalline solutions is recognized as a fairy-tale. It is here where the novels reveal their most unique capacity: to grasp the complex without simplifying it, to render the paradox without resolving it in a didactic tale."[2]

> "I have always felt that imaginative literature is an invaluable but untapped resource for executives trying to understand and resolve perennial human problems in business. . . . [Novels and plays] . . . do help us, though, to understand our basic needs and those of the people we manage: the need for identity, for self-esteem, for power, for control, for mental challenge, for acceptance, for security, for self-fulfillment, and for recognition.
>
> "These are the kinds of issues that do not go away by themselves. Nor can they be shunted off to Human Resources. They are problems that will recur even in the best of times, and changes in the way we do business will not mitigate them. Unattended to, they can derail our business strategies. They therefore require our ongoing personal attention."[3]

The Varieties of Leadership at Novarum Pharmaceuticals: A Novel, pages vii–x

Despite the power of storytelling as a teaching aid, business education tends to neglect it. Instead, it has long had a reputation for a narrow, technical approach to students' education. It seems that every day there are new headlines about business professionals who have lost their ethical way and confused the interests of their organizations or society with their own, or lost sight of their own humanity. Business schools have responded with courses in ethics, which students often regard as just another curriculum requirement.

Many college-level teachers supplement their management courses with cases designed to foster discussion and bring the issues of leadership and organizational behavior (L&OB) to life in the minds of their students. Many of us have been dismayed to find the students treating these cases not as inspiration for lively class discussions but as exercises—just another collection of items that may appear on an exam.

Trying to find a way to make case studies more engaging, I discovered that students responded readily to published fiction: stories like *Bonfire of the Vanities*, *Bright Lights, Big City*, or *Disclosure*, all of which depict organizational life in action. While such stories raised the level of student engagement, they were limited because ultimately they were not clearly centered on L&OB.

What is needed is a novel with interesting and sympathetic characters and a story driven by the principles of L&OB. This novel raises issues of L&OB in a way that is engaging but focused. It will be particularly valuable to undergraduates, who rely most heavily on education to prepare them for the world of work and who always get the rudest awakenings moving from the classroom to the office. Students will learn what it feels like to make various decisions in a corporate setting. They will come to class with a desire to know how the characters might have better controlled their situations. An astute instructor can channel this desire toward an informative discussion and learning experience. The novel, in other words, will become a kind of "practice" for day-to-day life in a corporation.

Writing fiction is not in the skill set of the typical management professor and business consultant. Fortunately, the co-author of this book is a multiskilled writer of fiction and nonfiction. Floyd Kemske is an editor, writing instructor, technical writer, marketing director and, perhaps most relevant for this project, the author of several published books of corporate fiction.[4] *Novarum Pharmaceuticals* is the result of our 5-year collaboration.

This book takes a fresh approach to teaching L&OB. It makes moral, interpersonal, and business problems immediate and real, demanding that students think about them in the same way they will one day face them in the workplace. In short, this book restores humanity to business education by stimulating student thinking about organizational behavior and human behavior at work in a globalized—sometimes dangerous—strategically challenging, and ethically debatable world.

Novarum Pharmaceuticals embodies all the elements of a novel, but unlike most novels, this one contains an index that professors and students alike can use to tie characters' actions to theory. The Instructor's Resources at the end of each chapter provide an extensive discussion framework for the professor, with background material on the pharmaceutical industry, biographical sketches of the principle characters, questions and suggested answers for every chapter, embedded descriptions of theory and concepts, learning goals for each chapter, and a bibliography and filmography of organization-related fiction. *Novarum Pharmaceuticals* will make a refreshing supplemental text in many courses within the undergraduate and graduate degree programs in business administration, psychology, sociology, organization development, public administration, health care management, and educational administration. General business readers interested in the consequences of mistakes and bad leadership will also find the book useful.

We hope to eventually create an interactive Web site that will deliver a real-time resource for students and instructors. In the meantime, we would greatly appreciate hearing from you and your students in the old-fashioned way—e-mail. Please direct your questions, anecdotes, requests for help, rants, and successes with *Novarum Pharmaceuticals* to Rob Pernick at rpernick@jhu.edu or Floyd Kemske at fkemske@thirdlion.com. We promise a speedy response.

We thank Dr. Phil Phan, Associate Dean at the Carey Business School of Johns Hopkins University, who introduced us to George Johnson, the forward-thinking publisher of Information Age Publishing, Inc. George had the imagination to include a new genre of work in IAP's stable of esteemed academicians. We are delighted to share this book with our colleagues and students.

Robert Pernick, PhD
Professional Faculty [management]
Carey Business School
Johns Hopkins University
Columbia, Maryland
Summer, 2009

Notes

1. Waldo, D. (1968). *The novelist on organization and administration.* Berkeley, CA: Institute on Government Studies.
2. Czarniawski-Joerges, B., & de Monthoux, P. G. (Eds.). (1994). *Good novels—better management: Reading organizational realities in fiction.* Chur, Switzerland: Harwood Academic Publishers.
3. Brawer, R. (1998). *Fictions of business: Insights on management from great literature.* New York: Wiley.
4. Kemske's novels are cited in the bibliography.

Introduction

The Varieties of Leadership at Novarum Pharmaceuticals: A Novel is set in a large U.S. corporation, and it follows the struggles of an executive vice president trying to launch an innovative project through a Middle Eastern company. The story proceeds from Nia Stevens's first strategic proposal for the joint venture, through various triumphs and setbacks, to a final crisis in which she must choose between what she views as her career and her principles. Stevens, like CEO Allan Hanna, CFO Ward Alexander, board member Eleanor Marcus, and CIO Rasheed Madhdabi, attempt to thrive in a company coping with the fundamental concerns of modern organizations: making smart strategic decisions in a richly connected, hypercompetitive global marketplace, managing demographic diversity, and leading ethically.

The challenges facing Nia and her Novarum colleagues are designed to inspire readers to think about and discuss issues affecting the lives of managers and professionals in any organization. Readers will find themselves coming to grips with questions such as: What criteria do decision makers use to hire, fire, and set compensation? What motivates a firm to outsource work and with what consequences? What are the boundaries between friendship and sharing confidential organizational information? What is a fair claim on an employee's time in an "always on" work world? What standards should employees use to reconcile their loyalty to themselves, their company, and society? These are the kinds of questions you and I live with every day, but there are no easy answers.

The Varieties of Leadership at Novarum Pharmaceuticals: A Novel, pages xi–xiii

The principal characters reveal a mix of motives and perceptions. Each has their own agenda and distinct worldview. They converge and clash around an important strategic decision facing the corporation, and their actions and reactions change as the story unfolds. It is said that in the logic of Hollywood, even a tragedy must have a happy ending. Novarum is not a Hollywood production and, as is often the case in organizational life, is neither a tragedy nor a comedy. Rather, it is a plausible depiction of life within an office, told in story form. As a story, it aims to teach several practical lessons for organizational leaders and staff alike. Among these lessons are the following:

- **Tell the Truth:** Small lies of omission and commission add up, putting the individual and organization on a dangerous trajectory.
- **Look Inside:** Unawareness—willful or unconscious—of one's emotions lessens self-control and predisposes one to act foolishly. Effective leaders have the self-confidence to admit their lesser angels.
- **Look Around:** Isolated leaders often fail. Postindustrial leaders collaborate with peers and are very open to being influenced by followers.
- **Look Outside:** Our human tendency to favor the familiar is clashing with the unprecedented, sudden, and massive encounter of peoples from different ethnicities, religions, nations, and culture. In a 21st-century economy, we have no choice but to move beyond tolerance to embracing "the other."
- **Treat Employees Fairly:** Valid surveys routinely report that a disturbingly large percentage of the employee population is disengaged from their jobs, leaders, and organizations. More worrisome, even engaged employees are about two episodes of insensitive treatment away from disgruntlement. It is not uncommon for disgruntled employees to behave in all sorts of devious ways to restore balance. We know that two wrongs don't make a right, but we've also witnessed immature, dysfunctional behavior from workers who perceive a breach in their psychological contract with the organization. Superiors need not be saints to gain employee compliance; but leaders must display respect if they hope to attract and keep the loyalty of followers.

In summary, *The Varieties of Leadership at Novarum Pharmaceuticals: A Novel* is a cautionary tale about the consequences of bad leadership, but with an important difference. Many popular books in this genre are brief and easily digestible, but nutritionally suspect. At 45,000 words, this story is also brief, but readers will appreciate its nuanced treatment of leadership. The characters are believable and their behavior familiar to anyone who has spent much time in a formal organization. The moral is clear: inattention to common human failings of excessive ambition, pride, misperceptions, and cognitive limits can cause organizations financial loss and damage employees' careers. Immersing yourself in this book will give you a deeper appreciation of the often conflicted nature of worker motivation. Thus prepared, you are better positioned to make thoughtful responses to the many important decisions you will face in your career.

Résumés of Principal Characters

Allen H. Hanna, MD, PhD, Chief Executive Officer

Age: 51

Hometown: Chicago, IL

Education:

- BS: Biology, Northwestern University, Evanston, IL
- MD: Columbia University, New York
- Residency (pediatric orthopedics): Brigham & Women's Hospital, Boston, MA

Employment Highlights:

- University of Rochester Hospital. Surgeon. Tenure: 5 years
- GlaxoSmithKline. Research scientist juvenile diabetes.Tenure: 6 years
- Johnson & Johnson, New Brunswick, NJ: EVP, Research & Development. Tenure: 7 years
- Novarum Pharmaceuticals. COO. Tenure: 3 years; CEO. Tenure: 2 years

Personal:

- Married, two children.
- Offline interests: handball, golf, competitive bridge.

The Varieties of Leadership at Novarum Pharmaceuticals: A Novel, pages xv–xviii

Nia O'Shaughnessy Stevens, PhD
Executive Vice President—Strategy

Age: 45

Hometown: Boston

Education:

BS Chemistry and Sociology, Reed College, Portland, OR

PhD Health Services and Policy Analysis, University of California at Berkeley

Employment Highlights:

Portland Biosciences Research Institute. Director, Epidemiology. Tenure: 4 years

Parisi Laboratories, S.p.A. Indianapolis, IN. Vice president, Account-Based Markets. Tenure: 6 years

Galenic Pharmaceuticals, Chicago, IL. VP, Emerging Markets. Tenure: 5 years

Novarum Pharmaceuticals, Chicago, IL. EVP Strategic Planning. Tenure: 2 years

Personal:

Divorced, one child

Offline interests: marathon running, glider piloting

Ward T. Alexander, MBA, CPA
Chief Financial Officer

Age: 48

Hometown: Richmond, VA

Education:

BS: Accounting, University of Richmond, VA (CPA Virginia and Michigan)

EMBA: Finance, University of Michigan Ann Arbor

Employment Highlights:

Kaiser Permanente. Director of Accounting, Mid-Western Region. Tenure: 5 years

Arthur Andersen, LLP. Healthcare Practice Manager, Asian Division. Tenure: 16 years

Novarum Pharmaceuticals. Role: CFO, Tenure: 4 years

Personal:

Married, two children.

Offline interests: walking, master chess player.

Eleanor Santos-Marcus, MPH, MD
Member, Board of Directors

Age: 59

Hometown: Albuquerque, NM

Education:

BS Physics, University of Colorado, Boulder, CO

M.D. University of Arizona, Tucson, AZ

Residency (orthopedics): Harvard University, Cambridge, MA

Employment Highlights:

Chief of Residents, Brigham and Women's Hospital, Boston, MA. Tenure: 5 years

Associate Professor of Medicine, Tufts University, Boston, MA. Tenure: 6 years

Chair, Department of Orthopedics, Tufts University, Boston, MA. Tenure: 10 years

University of Chicago School of Medicine. Role: Dean. Tenure: Present

Board of Directors: Novarum Pharmaceuticals. Tenure: 2 years

Personal:

Married, two children.

Offline interest: team captain, Chicago Rowing Club; board member, South American Archaeology Society

---

Rasheed A. Madhdabi, MS
Chief Information Officer

Age: 38

Hometown: Detroit, MI

Education:

BS Computer Science, Wayne State University, Detroit, MI

MS/MBA [Joint program] Computer Science & Business

Management, Michigan State University, East Lansing, MI

Employment Highlights:

Senior Information Technology Analyst, European/Middle-Eastern Division, Ford Motor Company, Dearborn, MI. Tenure: 7 years

Assistant Director, Administrative Computing, University of Toledo, OH. Tenure: 5 years

Director, Information Services, Novarum Pharmaceuticals, Chicago, IL. Tenure: 1 year

CIO, Novarum Pharmaceuticals, Chicago, IL. Tenure: 1 year

Personal:

Single, no children.

Offline interests: computer gaming, chapter president Audubon Society of Chicago

---

Reynold Bourdain, MD

Age: 52

Hometown: Paris, France

Education:

BS Biochemistry, Claude Bernard University, Lyon

MD University of Chicago

Residency (Orthopedic Surgery) Brigham & Women's Hospital, Boston

Fellowship (sports medicine) Southern Illinois University

Employment Highlights:

Staff physician, Chicago Bears NFL. Tenure: 15 seasons

Founder and Director, Greater Chicago Sports Medicine Center. 1990 to present

Personal:

Married, three children

Offline interests: handball, sailing

Prologue: "Do You Need a Ride?"

In 1989, the U.S. Postal Service assigned the headquarters of Rotare Pharmaceuticals, Inc. its own zip code. How could it have done otherwise? The 36-acre campus had its own Post Office, as well as a library, transportation service, drycleaners, gas station, drugstore, and bank. It also boasted no less than four restaurants, from an Au Bon Pain near the Administrative building to an intimate dining room located in the luxuriously appointed building known as Executive Place. The special dining room, which was known for its nouvelle cuisine, was said to be worthy of five stars in *North Carolina Monthly*, if only Rotare's management had allowed anyone from the magazine to eat there and review it. The campus was, in short, nearly self-sufficient—certainly better able to meet its own needs than was any of the five zip codes surrounding it.

In 1992, three years after the award of the zip code, Rotare Pharmaceuticals considered Ward Alexander for the position of Controller of its Finosec Division, named for its most successful product. Ward had no particular experience in pharmaceutical manufacture, but he had spent 16 years as the General Manager of Healthcare Practice for Arthur Andersen Asia. Rotare was looking to expand more aggressively into international markets, so his Asian experience had gotten their attention.

For his part, Ward had grown tired after 16 years of Hong Kong and wary about the changeover to Chinese rule, so on the strength of four weeks' accumulated vacation time, he had taken an apartment in Baltimore for a

The Varieties of Leadership at Novarum Pharmaceuticals: A Novel, pages xix–xxvi month and moved stateside with his wife to test his marketability among some of the larger health care companies.

Ward was impressive on paper, and Rotare bit almost immediately. He had an initial interview by phone with the company's CFO, whose name was Jack, and two days later flew down to North Carolina, on Rotare's dime, for an interview in person. Jack was as friendly and entertaining in person as he was on the phone. He was himself from Baltimore originally, and to be honest, Ward and he spent most of the hour they were together talking about the Orioles, whose chances looked good that year. But it was still early in the season.

After his meeting with Jack, Ward spent an hour with the VP of Human Resources, whose name was Elke, and who treated him like her new best friend. He was feeling good about both the opportunity and his prospects of an offer when he flew back to Baltimore that evening.

In fact, Elke telephoned him the next day and asked him to return for a day and meet with some of the division's department heads as well as half a dozen managers who would be reporting to him, should he get hired. So he returned and spent a whole day on the Rotare campus. Ward was a good interview, and he could tell that the people he met were impressed. At midday, Jack took him to lunch, to a restaurant in the next town, not to one of the company's captive eateries, and they talked more about the Orioles. And when his interviews were finished in the afternoon, Elke spent 2 hours giving him a tour, showing him the Finosec Division's executive offices before taking him out to see more of the 36-acre campus and its 16 buildings.

She drove him around in a Jeep, pointing to futuristic buildings and talking expansively about recreational opportunities, intracampus transportation, and the seasonal changes of North Carolina's highlands. Ward thought it delightful that Executive Place was on Finosec Drive. That the company had named its major roadway after an ulcer medication bespoke a sort of innocent pride that he found engaging.

By the time he got back to Baltimore, in the late evening, he felt even better about his prospects—good enough to ask his wife how she would like living in North Carolina. Adrienne, who was even more tired of the Far East than he, said, "Do they speak English there?"

He wasn't really surprised when Elke called the next morning and asked him to come to one more interview.

"I have arranged two tickets, business class," she said. "We'd like you to bring your wife along. I've arranged an appointment for her with a local real estate agent while you are doing the last of your interviews. I hope you're willing to stay overnight. That way, you two can have dinner at our special dining room. They are featuring whortleberry glazed capon. You don't want to miss that."

Ward's taste usually ran to dishes more pedestrian than whortleberry glazed capon, but he thought Adrienne might enjoy it, and he agreed they would stay the night.

Elke said she would make a reservation for him on the executive level of the Marriott, which was right up the road.

When they got to the hotel, there were flowers in the room from Elke. Adrienne was impressed. "They must really want you."

Ward shrugged. "It looks that way, doesn't it?"

On Elke's advice, Ward asked the hotel concierge to arrange a car rental for Adrienne so, in the morning, she would be able to drive him to the Rotare campus. She could then go off to meet the real estate agent, returning to meet Ward at noon. Elke had asked her to come for lunch and meet the other division executives. This was not to be the whortleberry meal, she assured them. Their meal at the five-star dining room was meant for the two of them alone. Elke had arranged it that way, since she suspected—even over the phone Ward could almost hear her wink as she said this—they would have some things to talk over at the end of the day. Given Elke's confidence, Ward assumed they were actually going to make him an offer that day.

At the gate to the campus, the guard looked up Ward on a list that was fastened to his clipboard, then gave brief directions to Human Resources, which was a half-mile down Finosec Drive, then a left on Ibuprofen Avenue. The drive was on a wonderfully smooth and lightly traveled road, with deep green grass on either side that was obviously tended intensively. Ward enjoyed pointing out to Adrienne the landmarks that Elke had pointed out to him. He was beginning to look forward to working at this place.

At the Administration building, his wife stopped the car. He gave her a kiss, then opened the door. "Wish me luck." He reached into the backseat and retrieved his briefcase.

"You won't need it," said Adrienne.

He smiled broadly. It's a wonderful feeling to have a woman who believes in you.

Over the next 2 hours, shuttling about from conference room to conference room and from office to office, Ward met six more people. He asked for a business card from each one so he could get an e-mail address for sending a thank you note later that evening. The cards helped him remember names too, but none of the names are important enough to this story to set them down here.

The subject of his sixth interview walked him back to Elke's office.

At first, Ward thought a change had come over Elke. She seemed preoccupied and looked at him as if she hadn't yet been introduced to him. But she snapped out of it in a moment and then resumed her sunny demeanor. "You're in luck, Ward," she said. "Our new CEO is on-site today. I didn't know if you'd be able to meet him, but he's back from his trip. His name is Suparman."

"Superman?" said Ward, wondering what a man had to do to excite such admiration among his staff.

"No." Elke did not smile. "Suparman. It's Javanese."

Ward remembered that Java was part of Indonesia, and then he remembered everyone saying the company wanted to be aggressive about international business.

"There's a car downstairs that will take you to Executive Place," she said.

Ward nodded. "My wife is supposed to meet me here at noon."

He wasn't certain, but he thought Elke colored for a moment.

Then she smiled. "I'm sure you'll be finished in time."

"May I leave my briefcase here?" he said.

"Better take it with you." She offered no additional explanation, and Ward didn't press it.

She hustled him out of her office, and as Ward climbed into the waiting air conditioned limousine, he realized he hadn't asked her how he should get back to the Administration building.

He leaned toward the front seat and the uniformed driver. "Do you know how I will get back?"

The driver looked back briefly. He shook his head. "Sorry."

Ward settled back in the seat and resolved not to worry about it. So far, every time he had been stuck in this process, the next step had always appeared, as if by magic, owing to Elke's careful and thoughtful planning.

The ride to Executive Place was brief. When he was ushered into Suparman's office, a short man with a round, dark face surmounted by horn-rimmed glasses approached him and shook his hand.

"I'm glad to meet you, Mr. Suparman," said Ward.

Suparman smiled. "Suparman is not a surname, Mr. Alexander."

"I'm sorry," said Ward.

"No need to be." Suparman gestured toward a sofa on the other side of the room, and the two of them walked over to it. "Many Javanese have only one name. Some of my countrymen adopt a second one for the sake of putting westerners at ease, but that is not one of my priorities."

Ward liked the man's civilized frankness. "What should I call you?"

"Suparman will do nicely," said the CEO.

"And you can call me Ward, please."

The two of them sat at opposite ends of the sofa.

"I understand you managed the Healthcare Practice for Arthur Andersen Asia," said Suparman.

"Yes."

"Tell me," said Suparman. "How many languages do you speak?"

Ward gave the question a moment's thought. "Two," he said. "English and Finance."

Suparman smiled. "How droll."

Ward was pleased to have amused him.

"I wonder, however," said Suparman, "how you could run the Asian division of a major corporation without learning Chinese."

Ward wondered if Suparman knew what the general manager of an overseas subsidiary does.

"I had to master English," said Ward, "in order to deal with our customers, nearly all of whom were overseas subsidiaries of American and multinational firms."

"Pity," said Suparman.

Ward was beginning to get a bad feeling. "Would my lack of Chinese count against me in being considered for this job?"

"Heavens, no," said Suparman. "I speak only a smattering of Chinese myself."

Ward felt mildly relieved.

"No," said Suparman, "it's a lack of interest in learning Chinese that might count against you."

Ward's relief evaporated, and he felt his ears burn.

"Our strategic plan," said Suparman, "is based on the aggressive pursuit of international trade. The leadership of our firm needs to be at least mildly curious about other cultures. Someone who is immersed in a foreign culture for more than a decade without picking up any of the language . . ." His voice trailed off to give Ward the opportunity to imagine for himself what Suparman thought of the monolingual.

Ward decided he didn't like Suparman after all. He mustered his dignity. "I guess there's not much point in continuing this meeting."

"I'm sorry." Suparman stood and offered Ward his hand. "Thank you for your time. I wish you the best of luck."

Ward didn't know what to say. He shook the man's hand, picked up his briefcase, and left.

Suparman made no move to help him find his way out.

But Ward knew he wanted to go down to the lobby, so in the corridor, he pressed the button to summon the elevator. He assumed he would find Elke waiting for him in the reception area to give him a kiss-off, or maybe the driver would be there to take him back to Human Resources so he could meet Adrienne. He would take the opportunity to tell Elke that they wouldn't be hanging around for the whortleberry glazed whatever.

But when he arrived in the lobby, there was no one there except the security guard at the reception desk, who asked him to surrender the temporary ID badge she'd given him 15 minutes before. Ward handed it over. "Will the car be coming for me?" he said.

The security guard shrugged and studied the monitor of the closed-circuit video system.

There didn't seem to be much choice. Ward walked out into the sunlight. There were a couple dozen cars parked in front of the building, but they were all empty. He stood in front of the building, looking up and down the road for a moment. What was he going to do? It was still an hour before his wife was supposed to meet him at Human Resources. And he couldn't imagine killing any part of that hour with anyone from Rotare's Human Resources department. He knew without being told that Elke had abandoned him. The lunch with the other executives had been called off. As for the whortleberry dinner, well he didn't like fancy food very much anyway.

It looked like his best hope was to meet his wife at the gate and save her the embarrassment of going to Human Resources to ask about him. He looked at the sun-baked asphalt of Finosec Drive ahead of him.

Well, it couldn't be more than a mile. He shrugged and set off down the left side of the roadway. There was no sidewalk.

He wondered how he must look—a short, solitary, balding man walking along this bucolic road in the sun, holding a briefcase. He looked down to make sure he wasn't swinging it. Might as well look serious for the security cameras that were no doubt trained on him.

What just happened, anyway? He couldn't help but feel he was the victim of an elaborate practical joke—that Rotare was never considering him for the job but just romancing him to set him up for this long walk down Finosec Drive. It took him a while to mentally work his way back from that precipice. Rotare had spent upwards of five thousand dollars on this series of interviews. Nobody spends five thousand dollars to treat a person spitefully.

As a corporate finance guy, Ward understood that what appeared to be willful in a corporation was often the result of randomness. The person in charge of spending five thousand dollars to interview a candidate wasn't making the decision to hire that candidate. The person making the decision to hire the candidate didn't know about the money that had been spent. And Ward knew that right now, Elke was back in her office trying to think of some way to make sure Suparman never found out how much the company had spent on flying Ward back and forth between Baltimore and North Carolina.

No, you couldn't take a corporation's actions personally. A corporation might be a legal person, but its actions were those of someone with a personality disorder—sometimes monumentally self-interested, sometimes self-sabotaging, always morally opaque.

He was gradually aware of a minivan, painted in Rotare corporate colors, driving along on the opposite side of the road, matching his speed. He looked at the driver.

The driver wore a business suit but was obviously a security type. He wore aviator sunglasses and appeared to be looking at Ward, although Ward couldn't see his eyes.

"Do you need a ride?" said the driver.

Ward knew the man wasn't offering him a ride out of kindness. He was offering him a ride because his security ethic was offended at having a lone man walking down this road, even one in a business suit. He wanted Ward off his campus and order restored.

At this point, Ward would have been glad of a ride, because he was bald, and he could feel the sun on his head. But even with all his thinking about the amorality of corporations, he still felt the need to stand on his dignity in his dealings with this poor excuse for a company.

"No, thanks." He glanced up into the brilliant blue of the cloudless sky. "It's such a beautiful day."

The security man said nothing, but his minivan accelerated and left Ward to walk alone again.

Ward watched the back of the van as it pulled away. He hoped he would not get sunstroke.

1

Doing Business with Terrorists

Nia set her sleeping laptop and her booklets on the table. She took a chair across from where Allen was sitting and said hello. She was rewarded with one of his incandescent smiles. The alert eyes, so dark they appeared black, sparkled as his smile crinkled the skin around them. He was always perfectly groomed, and he dressed like a mannequin at a high-market men's store. That, together with his handball-honed physique, made Nia often joke to herself that Allen Hanna was a male fashion model masquerading as the CEO of a large pharmaceuticals company. His studious, thoughtful leadership of Novarum Pharmaceuticals made the joke just that much funnier.

Nia had been looking forward to this meeting for weeks. Her duties as executive vice president included many functions, but the one she prized—the one she'd been trained for—was strategic planning. She had, in fact, taken this job because it was an opportunity to build a strategic planning function from the ground up. She'd been reasonably happy as the VP of emerging markets at Galenic Pharmaceuticals when Eleanor called her some 2 years ago. Eleanor sat on Novarum's Board. Novarum had no strategic planning function before Nia arrived, and Eleanor had convinced Allen

The Varieties of Leadership at Novarum Pharmaceuticals: A Novel, pages 1–26

of the value of hiring a strategic planner. He then hired Nia on Eleanor's recommendation.

Nia liked Allen, and during the first year liked the company. But over the past year, she had found it difficult to move such a large organization toward a longer-term outlook. However, she'd persevered and the result, finally, was this meeting.

This meeting was the last in a series of updates on Nia's strategic project. Allen had agreed to let it go forward, but she felt that it was in her best interest to update him regularly and bring him into the process. Her plan was to gain his permanent support by getting his participation. She thought of it with a certain amount of satisfaction as her personal strategic plan. She was going to be the one who finally got this company to look at forces outside its own industry and to think about long-term concepts like product life cycles. And while success would be good for its own sake (success always is), it would also validate what she and Eleanor only half-humorously called the "old girls network" that had brought her here.

Having taken her seat, she realized with some frustration she was facing the window. Somewhere in the distant past, Novarum's architect had given the CEO's office western exposure, and the afternoon sun would be shining in her face before the meeting was over. With the sun behind him, she wouldn't be able to see Allen's expression. Nia felt a blind meeting was worse than no meeting, a principle she held so strongly that she even refused to conduct significant business virtually. No matter how robust the IT medium, some nonverbal communication was always lost.

Ward entered and took a seat diagonally across from Nia at the small table. Novarum's CFO, Ward Alexander was a paunchy man with a plain face, the most prominent feature of which was a pair of glasses with large, rose-colored lenses. Nia had not known such eyewear existed outside the proverb, but Ward apparently wore them for some reason other than to bolster his optimism. He was also quite bald and had always looked to Nia like a character in a television sitcom. He was apparently not unaware of this impression, because he often cracked jokes and offered humorous asides in executive meetings, a practice that Nia recognized as a disguise for an otherwise ruthless defense of the company's bottom line. Short-term or long-term, it was all the same to Ward, and he'd sent many an innovative business idea off to oblivion with a well-placed bit of ridicule.

Unfortunately for the company's innovators, he was sharp as he was funny-looking. With Ward to her right and Allen directly across from her, Nia already felt like she might be vulnerable to a pincer movement—like the Romans facing Hannibal at Cannae. They lost 50,000 troops to that maneuver. At least she could make sure she didn't have the sun in her eyes. She casually rose and walked past Allen to the window, where she grabbed the cord and closed the curtains.

"Afraid of spies in helicopters?" said Ward.

"Yeah, right."

Allen and Ward laughed.

The content-free expression "Yeah, right" is the Swiss Army Knife of business conversation. You can answer nearly any remark with it and you will be thought ironic and witty. So Nia used it often. She thought witty and ironic were qualities that might play well in a strategic planner.

As she returned to her chair and sat, Allen tugged his cuff a few centimeters from the face of his watch and glanced at it. "Your meeting, Nia."

Nia nodded, took her booklets, and dealt them to Allen and Ward, keeping one for herself. "The team from Temel Ilac A.S. will be here tomorrow to make their presentation on the EA-311 project. I just wanted to brief you both on their company before the meeting." She held up her booklet. "This is their last year's annual report."

Allen looked at his copy in apparent disbelief, but Ward glanced at the cover and smiled.

"Yeah, right." He laughed.

Nia'd had the same reaction herself when she'd seen the thin pages with their slightly out-of-register two-color printing. Temel Ilac came out of a different sort of tradition, one that apparently didn't shovel much of the company's resources annually into a criminally overproduced public relations showcase.

"They need a new art director and a new production manager," she said, "but their numbers are good."

Allen shook his head in apparent wonder. "Are they serious? What do their investors think? How can you do business with such a cheesy annual report?"

"Cheesy." Ward held it out in front of him and laughed. "It's still got some curds sticking to it."

"Kurds?" said Nia.

Ward stopped laughing. "You know. Cheese. Curds."

"Oh. I thought you were talking about an ethnic group."

Ward looked embarrassed and Nia put a point up on her mental scoreboard.

"Heaven forbid," he mumbled.

No one laughed.

Nia thought with satisfaction that she had neutralized Ward for the time being. She resolved to keep an eye on him. She had made him feel guilty, but prodding him any further about it could convert his guilt to resentment, and that would be dangerous. In any meeting, Nia liked to know the brinks, and she felt she already had Ward standing at one. He could go either way from here: ally or enemy.

She looked at Allen. "I imagine the investors care more for the company's mission than its art direction."

Allen nodded as if he could respect this. He looked closely at the cover of the annual report. "Tell me again what this name means."

Nia nodded. "Temel Ilac A.S. roughly translates into 'Main Pharmaceuticals, Inc.' They do business throughout the Middle East."

Allen said nothing, but he pursed his lips in apparent thought.

"But Turkey's a European country, right?" said Ward.

"The Middle East is a congenial market for many Turkish firms. The Islamic connection eases the way in for them."

This seemed to rouse Allen from his thoughtfulness. "Islamic? You mean these guys are Muslims? Why are they anything? I thought Turkey was a secular country."

"That's right," said Nia. "The Turkish constitution even outlaws religiously based political parties. But the country is ninety-eight percent Muslim and Islam is a part of the country's history. It's difficult to say just how religious a country Turkey is. Most knowledgeable observers see Turks as more intensely nationalistic than religious. After all, the medieval Anatolians never chose Islam; it was imposed on them by the Seljuqs. Still, as in many countries, including ours, religion is strongest in the countryside. Istanbul, where Temel Ilac is headquartered, is a cosmopolitan city, not significantly more religious than, say, Baltimore. The management of Temel Ilac is working on an agenda no different than ours. They want to deliver a value proposition to customers and conform to good business practices."

Nia watched Allen as she fed him this background. He was clearly listening. That was one of his most reliable characteristics. He always listened. She decided she could risk injecting some philosophy.

"Globalization is many things," she said, "but it's animated by the norms of profit-seeking enterprises. In this respect, Temel Ilac is just like Novarum. They make decisions to advance profits, not doctrine. As one of the executives confided to me, 'religion may be a problem, but it is not what Turkey is.'"

It was a good lead-in to her presentation, so she pulled the laptop over in front of her and raised its lid to wake it. Her PowerPoint presentation was already cued up. She began to turn the machine so they could all see the screen when Allen reached across the table. He gently pushed the lid back down.

"Before we get to that, Nia," he said, "let's look at the rationale for this project again. Tell me why we need to outsource the development and testing of EA-311 to a company in another country."

Nia was taken aback. "I thought we had agreed on this."

"I said if you put together a good enough proposal, we would do it," said Allen. "But I need to see if you have covered everything."

Nia remembered the conversation differently, but she saw the futility of arguing with him. If Allen wasn't sold on the project, it wasn't going to happen. He was apparently a man who must be resold several times before the deal goes through.

"You realize, of course, that developing and testing a pharmaceutical costs a lot less in Turkey than it does here." She glanced at Ward.

"That might make Ward smile," said Allen, "but money isn't the only consideration in a decision like this."

"Of course it isn't." Nia fought to keep the bristles out of her voice. "But it's the consideration that makes all the other considerations possible."

"That's what I want," said Allen. "The other considerations."

"First," said Nia, "Turkey is currently one of the world's best markets for a birth control preparation. The Turkish Family Health and Planning Foundation has operated there since the 1980s, and they have gotten a fairly conservative culture to open up to the idea of birth control, mostly by a gently humorous advertising campaign for their own brand of condoms. The Turks are very traditional about family planning, but a recent poll showed that two thirds of married Turkish women don't want any more children. In fact, the Turkish government reluctantly concedes that family planning is a big social and economic problem. Rather than creating a need, Novarum will be fulfilling a need."

"What about the religion?"

"That's the most beautiful part," said Nia. "When several developing countries started flirting with family planning programs in the 1970s, they were careful to bring the Muslim clerics on board. They justified birth control with teachings from the Q'uran. They even issued a fatwa for the IUD in the early 1980s. Islamic law isn't operative in Turkey, but the support of the clerics makes it more acceptable to all Muslims. And this gives us a foothold from which to move into markets where Sharia matters more."

Ward spoke up again. "What's Sharia?"

"Islamic law based on the Q'uran," said Nia.

"Like Church law?"

"Not exactly," said Nia. "It covers civil and criminal matters as well as religious ones. In fact, it's one of the world's three great traditions of jurisprudence. It ranks with common law and civil law." Nia sensed she was starting to lecture, so she cut herself off and watched Ward and Allen for their reactions.

Ward nodded. Allen was impassive.

"It sounds like they're a good market," said Ward. "Could we develop the product here and just sell it there?"

"That's the other thing that makes Turkey so attractive," said Nia. "Given the current political situation here, it's dangerous for us to develop a new birth control product domestically. Now that American fundamentalists have managed to shut down abortion clinics in something like ninety percent of U.S. counties, they are looking for something else to protest. Abortions are on the decline, and they have to find a new focus if they're going to keep their movement alive. That new focus is going to be birth control."

"I don't believe that," said Ward. "Most women in this country use birth control. They aren't going to stand for it."

"That's what we said about abortion too."

"She's right about the fundies," said Allen. "You should see my mail. They don't like OviMate. They threaten me about it all the time." He turned to Nia. "Why should the fundies be any less angry about our developing a birth control drug in Turkey?"

"I've looked into this," said Nia. "These people pay very little attention to anything that happens outside the United States. Sometimes they get wound up a little about China or Africa, but Turkey is entirely off their radar. It's very safe."

"You seem to have an answer for everything, Nia," said Allen.

Nia could feel her face pulling itself into a smile. All her preparation was beginning to pay off. This thing was going to happen. "Well, then," she said. She opened the laptop again.

Again, Allen reached over and pushed the lid shut. "I don't need to be dazzled by your PowerPoint," he said. "Just tell us what to expect from these guys tomorrow, and tell us how strong you think their company's candidacy is."

She started to raise the laptop's lid again. "That's what the slides are for."

But a frown started to gather on Allen's face like thunderheads in the distance.

"Yes, well . . ." Nia closed the laptop again. She'd spent weeks on those slides, and some of them were utterly beautiful. And how could she present her argument without her presentation? Irritation welled up in her like warm champagne in the neck of a magnum.

As if he'd read her mind, Allen prodded her gently. "You must know the broad contours of this thing. That's all I'm interested in. You can e-mail the PowerPoint to Ward if it has numbers he can't find in their annual report."

Ward nodded. With the two of them unified on this, the pincer movement would be underway momentarily.

"Just tell me why you like these guys," said Allen.

Nia examined the question for hidden traps. There didn't seem to be any, so she took a breath and started. "I like them because they know this market better than we could even hope to. They are skilled, which you can see from their track record in product development. The top management all speaks English. Finally, I think we have to keep a weather eye on the possibility of backlash over there too. So I like them because they are Muslim."

Nia gave the two men a few moments to digest her points. Allen, with his elbows on the arms of his chair, made a steeple of his forefingers and rested his chin on it. Ward looked through the flimsy pages of the Temel Ilac annual report.

Finally Allen spoke. "What's the difference between Turks and Arabs?"

Nia gave her answer as much seriousness as she thought the question deserved, which wasn't a great deal. "About the same difference you'd find between us and Latin Americans."

Allen seemed to take it at face value. He digested it, then after a pause, he spoke again. "I owe it to you to make sure you have all the information that could possibly bear on this. You may like them because they are Muslim, but that's just the reason I don't like them."

A black, musty feeling formed in Nia's stomach. She found it difficult to speak, and the first time she did, nothing came out of her mouth but a squeak. She cleared her throat and started again. "Allen, an outsider hearing this might think you were prejudiced. Or at a minimum, ethnic profiling."

He looked at her sadly. "I guess you could call it prejudice. I never told you about this before, but my frat brother and best man was a vice president for Cantor Fitzgerald. He was killed at the World Trade Center."

Nia instinctively reached across the table to touch his hand before she realized what she was doing and stopped herself. She pulled her hand back and clasped it with the other one on the table. "I'm sorry. But you must see that doesn't have anything to do with Temel Ilac. They're a drug company. They aren't terrorists. They aren't even Arabs."

"I worry," said Allen, "and I'm sure many of our employees would worry, that they might have connections to terrorists. Isn't Turkey a hotbed of terrorist activity?"

"Allen," she said, "why did you let me work on this project so intensively if you had already made up your mind to disapprove it?"

"Oh, I've made up my mind," said Allen. "But that doesn't mean I'm going to disapprove it. It just means you have to build a stronger case for it."

That was the frustrating thing about working for Allen. Whenever you thought you'd caught him being human, with ordinary human failings and feelings, it turned out to be another management technique. But it was still unfair. How could she marshal a strong enough case to overcome this kind of prejudice?

Then she thought about Hannibal at Cannae again. Outnumbered, he faced the finest military machine of its day. His elephants were all dead by then. He had to fight with his wits. He put the weakest part of his army in the center against the strongest part of the Roman army. When the Romans advanced, they rolled over Hannibal's center and kept on going. As they advanced deeply into his center, Hannibal folded his flanks, which held his strongest forces, around the Romans and attacked them from all sides. In effect, he turned the Roman army's advantage, its powerful advance, against them.

Was there any way to turn Allen's prejudice around?

"Allen," she said, "it sounds like you may believe we are at war with the Muslims. Muslim politics, like politics in all societies, is not monolithic. Differing interpretations of Islam occur due to a nation's history, geography, and leadership. I've done research on this and was surprised and pleased to learn that medieval Muslim society was religiously pluralistic. Christians, Jews, Hindus, others, lived alongside Muslims. Therefore, it's wrong to say that Muslims always engage in conflict with non-Muslims."

"I believe we are at war with the entire developing world, regardless of religion" he said. "There's a lot of hopelessness out there, and it breeds terrorism. Furthermore, I'm proud that Novarum is a good corporate citizen. I know that sounds sentimental, but I believe it. We don't do things without thinking carefully about the implications for our society."

"Then outsourcing EA-311 to Temel Ilac might be the best thing we can do right now to strike at Islamic terrorism," she said.

Allen looked at her skeptically.

"There's no evidence whatever that Temel Ilac has any terrorist connections," Nia went on. "But there is evidence that this could be a major deal for them. It would increase employment at their Turkish plants and laboratories, engage some of the educated minds in the Turkish Muslim community, and give these people a chance to prosper. You say there's a lot of hopelessness out there. Well, this is the best way to give people in a developing country hope. When you think about it, this is the only way to fight terrorism."

Having finished her little speech, she lapsed into silence. The only sound in the room was a faint click from the building's ventilation system. A cold draft blew on the top of her head. Nia felt like an Olympic gymnast waiting for her scores. She didn't take her eyes off Allen, who stared thoughtfully at the tabletop.

* * *

Ward was quite certain he had never been on a quiz show before, and yet his presence on this one felt like something he'd always done—like it was his job or something. Nor did it seem unusual to him that he was naked—uncomfortable, yes, but not unusual. The studio was very bright and at the periphery of his vision, he could see that not all the lights were white. Some were yellow, some red, some green, and so on. Many of them flashed, and it occurred to him that the show's organizers did this to distract him so he would find it more difficult to get the answers right. He waited for the emcee, who bore a strong resemblance to Nia Stevens from the office, to look up from the card she was holding.

"This is for the Grand Prize, Ward," she said.

Ward nodded.

"Rather than retire outstanding debt, a firm can choose to take it off the balance sheet by putting into escrow assets sufficient to cover it. What is this procedure called?"

Ward knew this. He had participated in such a procedure when he worked for Andersen. It is called defeasance.

"Five seconds, Ward," said Nia.

Ward smiled broadly and told her, or he thought he told her. She continued to look at him questioningly, and he realized that when he spoke nothing had come out.

"Three seconds, Ward," said Nia.

He tried to speak, but again there was no sound. He formed the first syllable with his tongue against the backs of his front teeth, but only silence emerged. He tried again. Nothing.

"Is that your final answer, Ward?" said Nia.

He tried to shout, but the result was the same.

"I'm sorry, Ward," said Nia.

A buzzer, jagged and jeering, sounded.

Ward woke up.

He was lying in bed. The bedroom was dark. His wife, Adrienne, was asleep beside him in the king-size bed. His heart was beating rapidly. What a strange dream. Was it supposed to be a nightmare? He felt no particular fear, just disappointment, even though he had no idea what the "Grand Prize" was supposed to be.

Then the buzzer sounded again, startling him. And although it was clearly the same sound that had buzzed him out of his dream, he realized it was much more familiar than that. It wasn't a buzzer at all. It was Adrienne's snore.

He lifted his head from the pillow, turned it, and looked over at her. Her dark shape was still. Past her, he could see the display of the clock radio: 4:10.

Defeasance. Why hadn't he been able to say it? And what was Nia Stevens doing in his dream? Then he remembered the meeting from the day before. She had jumped on him for making an ethnic joke when he hadn't even made one. Hadn't she ever heard of curds? Curd was practically a synonym for cheese. It had been one of the best jokes he'd ever made, and she spoiled it. Not only that, but she'd made it impossible for him to make any more jokes in the meeting. How can you joke with somebody who takes an off-topic remark as a slur on some group or other?

Nia was humorless, politically correct, and quick to take offense where none was intended. She was not the kind of person Ward ordinarily liked to work with. But she certainly could put together a large strategic project. After their meeting, he had studied her numbers for the EA-311 project and was amazed by them. Her project offered a better return on investment than the company's overall business, and it appeared to be nearly risk free. She'd made a believer out of him, so he had decided to speak with Allen today before Temel Ilac's presentation.

Allen's remark at the meeting echoed in his mind. Money isn't the only consideration in a decision like this. Ward would have to find a way to disabuse him of this notion. Nia's EA-311 project was so attractive, he didn't think Novarum could afford not to do it.

Now he realized he was not falling back to sleep. He had once read somewhere long ago that if you can't sleep, you should get out of bed. He'd read it so long ago that he couldn't remember the reasoning behind it. But that didn't matter, for he'd been following the rule so long that it was now habit. He shifted his legs quietly over the side of the bed then followed them with the rest of his body. He took his robe from where it hung over the back of the chair beside the bed. He put it on, slipped his feet into his slippers, donned his glasses and wristwatch from the bedside table, and padded down the stairs toward the kitchen. Part-way down the staircase, he heard the wrong-answer buzzer again and silently wished Adrienne a good sleep.

He made himself a cup of coffee and went into the den where he had set up a little office for the days he worked at home. He sipped at the coffee while he started up his computer and then logged on. He called up the day's headlines from the Internet to scan them for business implications, but it was the usual stuff: melting ice in Antarctica and at the North Pole, terrorist attacks in Iraq and Turkey, long-term interest rates on the rise, a swine flu outbreak in Mexico, tension between India and Pakistan as border troops were put on alert. One thing, however, caught his eye:

Court Documents Reveal
Ties Between Ford, Nazi Germany

The news story recounted that Ford had a successful subsidiary in Germany before World War II. When the Nazis came to power, Ford Germany cooperated with the Reich and manufactured vehicles for the Army, sometimes with forced labor. The subsidiary did good business, and the parent company benefited. Henry Ford was even given a medal by Adolf Hitler. It continued that way right up to the declaration of war. Now Ford was being sued by some of the people who had survived forced labor in its German factories.

Imagine being sued just for doing business the best way you knew how. How could the executives at Ford know the Reich would wind up at war with most of the world? And once the war got underway, how could they know it would lose?

He imagined the executives at Ford regretted their predecessors' decision not to sell off Ford Germany when the Nazis came to power. What a mess.

His in-tray was full of unpaid household bills, so he decided to retire some of those. He was a little old-fashioned and still insisted on writing checks for them rather than paying them online. He disliked the idea of sending any financial information over the Internet.

On top of the stack was a Visa bill for $1.88. He hadn't used the card to buy anything in the last month, but the company had posted this small charge. The bill said it was a finance charge, but he wondered how you could incur a finance charge when there was no principal amount to calculate it on. The bill said the amount due was $.00. Apparently $1.88 didn't reach some kind of minimum. If he let it go, it would just appear on next month's bill.

It probably wasn't even worth the time and effort of writing a check for it. And yet . . .

He still wondered where the charge came from.

He turned the bill over. There was an 800 number to call with questions, "24 hours a day." Why not? He dialed the 800 number.

The call was answered immediately (there weren't very many people trying to get through before dawn, after all), and the greeting message played.

"Please listen carefully to the choices, as they have recently changed. If you are calling to report a lost or stolen card, press one . . ."

The voice, which Ward thought he recognized as that of a film actress he had seen a few times in the movies, made him more patient with the voice-mail system than he might have been. He wondered how the Visa company could cost-justify hiring a well-known film actress for an outgoing telephone message. He had no idea what she might have cost, but he was certain there was no easy way to measure the return on investment.

The next menu asked him to enter his sixteen-digit account number on the telephone keypad. After he punched in the number, a synthesized voice spoke his name and asked him to confirm it. It occurred to him that if he'd entered the wrong number by accident, the voice would have given him another account holder's name. The same was true for anyone else using the system. He felt uncomfortable at the thought of this system speaking his name to some stranger.

Then he was connected to a human being. She spoke with an Indian accent over a faint but distinct line noise, and Ward suspected she was about six-thousand miles away. Her accent could have been Pakistani; he could never tell the difference. He wondered if she was anywhere near those troop buildups. She said her name was Becky.

"And what is the matter I may be helping you with today, Mr. Alexander?" said Becky.

Ward understood the international outsourcing game. Whether Becky answered Visa inquiries, listened to complaints about bugs in cereal, or took orders for collectible plates probably depended entirely on chance. Her computer doubtless put the appropriate script in front of her depending on the particular number her caller had dialed. Good for her. He was glad technology gave her the opportunity to make a good living. It was interesting that she knew far more about him than he knew about her. He didn't even know her real name.

"I have a problem with my bill."

"Indeed," she said. "What might be the difficulty you are having, Mr. Alexander?"

He pictured her sitting in a cubicle, wearing a headset, and probably a sari, with a keyboard and screen in front of her. "This month my bill shows no transactions whatever except for a finance charge of one dollar and eighty-eight cents," he said.

"I am seeing that charge, Mr. Alexander."

Ward got a cold feeling in the pit of his stomach. He was a CFO, and the sanctity of sensitive records was as good as encoded in his DNA. He could understand why it made business sense to outsource call centers, but it hadn't occurred to him until now that somebody on the other side of the world was fooling around with his financial records. What would the Visa company do if her office was overrun by some of those border troops? Would his records then become contraband of war?

"Becky," he said, "are you looking at my account statement right now?"

"Indeed, Mr. Alexander. May I be explaining to you the origins of this charge of one dollar eighty-eight?"

Ward didn't know what to say. He felt like asking her to close his file before the troops arrived. But that was silly, and he realized that ending the call could get her into trouble. For all he knew, the proprietors of this call center caned employees who allowed customers to get away without having their problems solved.

"Mr. Alexander?" said Becky. "May I be explaining to you the origins of this charge of one dollar eighty-eight?"

"Go ahead," said Ward absently.

"A variety of purchase and cash advance features are available on your account, Mr. Alexander. We calculate a portion of the finance charge on your account each day by multiplying the daily balance on each feature by the applicable daily periodic rate. We do this each day of the billing period, including the closing date. To get the daily balance, we take the beginning balance for each feature every day, add any new transactions, fees, and any finance charge on the previous day's balance, subtract any credits or payments credited as of that day, and make other adjustments. The balances subject to finance charge are the averages of the respective daily balances during the billing period. If you multiply this figure for each feature by the number of days in the billing period and by the applicable daily periodic rate, the result will be the periodic finance charge assessed for that feature, except for minor variations caused by rounding."

The situation was nothing if not remarkable. A personable young woman was reading a script to explain the procedure for calculating a finance charge to the CFO of a Fortune 500 pharmaceuticals firm. And as near as Ward could tell, the explanation had no relationship to his problem. It would have been funny if he weren't so troubled about the matter of his account information being vulnerable to foreign attack. You can't predict wars, but anybody knows where they are likely to occur. The newspapers tell you that. How could the Visa people be so shortsighted as to send his financial records to a country that might become a war zone at any moment?

"Mr. Alexander?"

Ward brought his mind back to the question at hand. "Yes?"

"I am seeing that your payment record is excellent." There was a pause.

Ward's discomfort would not go away. Some Indian woman, whose name might or might not be Becky, was looking at his gasoline purchases, movie rentals, and restaurant lunches. Then he realized the line had gone dead quiet. Had she hung up on him?

Seconds later, the faint line noise returned. Ward realized she had muted the line, probably to check with her supervisor.

"I am having the one-time authority to cancel this charge," she said at last, "which I would like to do, with your permission, Mr. Alexander."

Ward hesitated, but Becky charged ahead.

"In consideration of your excellent payment history, Mr. Alexander, I am to be authorizing the cancellation of this charge now."

He mumbled a "thank you" and hung up the phone.

He looked down at the Visa bill, still in his hand. Becky had cancelled the $1.88 charge, but she had never told him where it came from. He'd just had an experience with globalization, and he wasn't entirely comfortable about it. He might be $1.88 richer, but he felt exposed and uneasy. And he wondered if Turkey was on the verge of war with anyone.

* * *

Eleanor's schedule was clear for an hour after running her weekly meeting with the department chairs, so she thought it was a good time to try to talk with Allen Hanna. Nia had called her three days ago to tell her Allen, after greenlighting it at two different milestones, had cancelled the Turkish project. This move seemed foolish to Eleanor, and not just because she had a close mentoring relationship with Nia.

Allen was the CEO of Novarum Pharmaceuticals, but he did not seem to realize how vulnerable the company was. In an age of globalized competition, Novarum had almost no business outside the United States. Much of its business was based on the blockbuster Novarum, a patented tranquilizer that was the best in its market because of its efficacy and safety. But the patent was due to expire and, rather than aggressively developing new drugs to replace it, Allen's plan had been to reformulate it as NovarumRT and secure the vital new patent.

Allen's casualness about strategy concerned Eleanor. She could not seem to make him understand the magnitude of the risk.

"If our biggest cost is in development," she had said at the last Board meeting, "then that's where our biggest risk lies as well. We've been working on the reformulated Novarum for eight years, and you just told us it has cost half a billion dollars. What if the development fails?"

"How would it fail?" he said.

"It might not do what it's supposed to do. It might have unacceptable side effects. It might—"

Allen interrupted her. "Those aren't realistic possibilities. We have decades of experience with Novarum. In this case, development simply amounts to reformulating the preparation so it acts the way it has always acted but with measurably less gastric distress. The clinical trials are going very well."

Eleanor looked around at the other Board members. They were all watching her. From body language, she could tell she probably had the support of Fran Rasmussen, but the others were all either supporting Allen or undecided. In any case, nobody else was going to speak until they could determine which way the wind was blowing. Eleanor wasn't ready to give up yet.

"That's great news the trials are going well," she said. "But that's not relevant to the point I'm making here. I'm sure you and your team have done everything possible to minimize the risk. Nevertheless, there is a risk."

"There's always a risk in pharmaceuticals development," said Allen. "It's part of doing business."

"All I'm saying," said Eleanor, "is that if we reduce development costs, we reduce the risk."

Allen nodded toward Ward. "Ward keeps a pretty tight reign on costs as it is."

"I'm sure he does," said Eleanor. "But I was thinking of a more dramatic step."

This seemed to spark some interest around the table, and Eleanor could tell, as the other directors leaned toward her, that she had engaged them at some level. "I'm talking about biosimulation," she said. "We use computer modeling to capture everything that's known about a disease, down to the cellular level, and then test its reaction to different interventions. This could dramatically speed up the pace of experimentation. If you cut the time, you cut the costs."

Having rested her case, Eleanor waited for Allen's response. She sensed the other members of the Board looking toward him for an answer.

"That's a superlative idea," said Allen at last. "Do you have any background reading you could send me on this methodology?"

"Of course," said Eleanor.

"I want to read up on it so we can begin to think about doing it the next time we are working on a disease-specific treatment. This would be a very effective way to research a preparation for say, tuberculosis."

Eleanor could sense the "but" that was coming.

"But," said Allen, "I don't see what use it would be in creating tranquilizers. I doubt you can model depression at the cellular level."

Some of the Board members chuckled.

It had been impossible to discuss it any further after that, and Eleanor realized she had lost her main chance to bring in biosimulation through bad timing. Of course it was useless in developing tranquilizers! But it was making a place for small, undercapitalized firms to challenge giants like Novarum. And who knows? Maybe depression *was* a bacterial infection. Stranger discoveries had been made. And the day someone found the bacteria responsible for it was the day the tranquilizer business went away.

To conclude the meeting, Allen reiterated that he had studied the last several successful reformulations and he was certain of the strategy's success for NovarumRT. He believed the reformulated drug was unique and substantially different from the original Novarum.

At that meeting, he also floated the idea of entering the over-the-counter market with an acne medicine. Thankfully the Board nixed that idea as being too removed from Novarum's heritage and core competencies. Suggestions by the Board that Novarum should direct R&D funds to the chronic ailments of the enormous geriatric population went unheeded.

Nia's Turkish plan, on the other hand, held promise as a way of not only taking Novarum into a relatively new and certainly burgeoning market—Middle Eastern birth control—but also as a way to go international. Partnering with a successful Turkish firm would minimize risk and give Novarum's managers valuable experience in managing and marketing in a foreign culture. Nia stressed to Eleanor that first mover advantage would keep the competition at bay, particularly in an emerging market. Partnerships rely on trust and take time to grow, even within the same country. Avoiding cultural collisions across national borders is considerably more challenging than domestic mergers, as Eleanor recalled from the spectacularly unsuccessful Daimler-Chrysler hook up and divestiture. More than one Board member was handed her hat in the wake of that $30 billion bath.

Nia convinced Eleanor of the Middle Eastern strategy's soundness and that she had the change management skills to mesh the cultures. Potential entrants would have a hard time penetrating the market after Novarum's considerable—but culturally sensitive and legal—marketing and sales campaign established a presence. Nia even outlined a differential pricing plan based on each Middle Eastern country's GDP. In effect, the more wealthy nations would subsidize the poorer ones. Social justice, Nia called it. Sailing under a Turkish flag, Novarum could dominate the market. It seemed a winning strategy all around. Except Allen cancelled it.

Eleanor didn't think there was anything sinister behind Allen's decision. She'd known the man for a long time, and he'd always been straightforward and honest, if a little opinionated. Not unlike Nia, Eleanor had to grant. But most people with both an MD and a PhD were a little opinionated, and they tended to be convinced of the quality of their own insight. Allen just needed a little encouragement, delivered from the right person to change his perspective.

To provide this encouragement, Eleanor had quietly polled the other Board members and lined up majority support for a resolution to encourage Novarum to embark on an international project. She knew since Nia's project was in place and ready to be approved, he would probably reverse himself and approve it. That would be nice for her protégé, but it was less important than getting Novarum out of its provincial outlook and into the modern world. As she had explained to the other directors, the stockholders could interpret Novarum's isolationism as negligence. The members of the Board could be held personally liable, so Eleanor's cherry-picked majority was eager to go along with her resolution, and just as eager to have her informally notify Allen.

So she punched in his number and listened to the phone ring at the other end. It only rang once.

"Allen Hanna."

"Allen, it's Eleanor Marcus," she said. "Do you have a moment?"

She knew it was unusual for him to get a call from a member of the Board of Directors. Even Eleanor, the most active member of the Board, rarely called him. There was an unspoken agreement among Board members to do most of their business by e-mail. She had, in fact, used e-mail to sell him first on the idea of creating an executive level strategic planner position and second on filling it with Nia.

While she expected wariness, however, he seemed genuinely pleased.

"I'm delighted to hear from you, Eleanor."

"Well, maybe I will need more than just a moment," she said.

She heard clicking at the other end of the line and realized he was typing. That was one of the things she liked about Allen. He was a hands-on guy.

"Eleanor," he said over the typing, "I am typing a block into my calendar right now. What do you need? An hour? I am supposed to address the U.S. Senate in a few minutes, but they can wait."

She laughed and was pleased to find him in such a jocular mood.

"What can I do for you?" he said.

"Allen, I've been working with the other Board members to develop a plan we want you to consider for Novarum's future direction."

"Oh?"

Was that wariness in his voice?

"We have discussed this, and I have polled everyone. Five of the Board members support this plan."

There were eight members on the Board, counting Allen. With the reliable support of Tom Rafferty, that meant that Allen only ever had to gain the support of three other members in order to have majority support. But Eleanor had headed off that possibility.

"What's the plan, Eleanor?"

She felt like she was entering the negotiation phase of the conversation. She kept her voice as friendly as she could. "We've looked at the future, Allen, and we think in this competitive environment, Novarum needs to respond to globalization."

She paused to let him respond.

"We've set up an international marketing operation," he said.

"The Board doesn't feel that's enough," said Eleanor. "We think it's time to consider some international strategic alliances. We think Novarum should partner with a company in a developing country for the creation and marketing of a product."

"Oh?"

"We think it is a competitive step. And it's a long-term step. It's even important to global stability."

"Let me guess," said Allen. "Does the Board want to partner with a firm in Turkey?" There was no humor in the quip.

"Turkey sounds promising," said Eleanor. "But of course, the Board doesn't have the day-to-day experience and the hands-on contact that you have. We would leave it to you to work out the particulars. We just felt it was our responsibility to advise you of our feeling. If Novarum tries to act like it's not part of a global industry, shareholder value will suffer. And it's our responsibility, of course, to preserve shareholder value."

Eleanor knew she was playing a risky game here. She wasn't lying when she told him she had a majority of the Board behind her, but the supporters she had lined up had not heard from Allen yet. He could be very persuasive, and she could imagine him getting many of her majority to change their minds. It might look transparent for him to lobby them, but she was betting that he wouldn't be able to justify the effort of doing so, particularly given the rift it would obviously open on the Board. Nevertheless, if he chose to resist, he could probably prevail. He had, after all, selected nearly everyone in her majority for Board membership, including her. The gamble was that he would respond to this development as a responsible businessman rather than a man of pride. Allen knew as well as anyone you cannot run a Fortune 500 company by gratifying your ego, although there were many CEOs who tried.

"In fact, Eleanor," he said evenly, "we have been working here on a project to partner with a firm in Turkey."

It was only a small—what, distortion?—and it offered the opportunity for him to save face.

"Excellent," she said.

"Nia has prepared a PowerPoint on it," he said. "Would you like me to have her send you a copy?"

Now it was Eleanor's turn to lie. She already had a copy of Nia's PowerPoint.

"Yes, please," she said, "send it along."

They exchanged a few jokes and remarks about the weather and then agreed that they had taken enough of each other's time. Eleanor set the handset down to hang up. This project was the right thing for Novarum Pharmaceuticals and it was a good move for Nia. Ultimately, it would be a good move for Allen as well. He would be the CEO who brought Novarum into the global marketplace. Everything seemed right about it. Why did she feel so uneasy?

Instructor's Resources

Learning Goals

Based on reading this chapter and knowledge of leadership and organizational behavior theory, students will be able to

- provide explanations of employee perceptions and motives, leading to plausible predictions of future behavior
- recognize that business proposals are derived from strategic thinking
- explore some of the cultural, ethical, and perceptual complexities of launching a joint venture between a U.S. corporation and a Middle-Eastern firm in a post-September 11 world
- begin to examine how stereotypical thinking and religious discrimination influence decision making.

Discussion Questions and Possible Instructor's Responses

Q**1** ***Using popular organizational behavior theories, how would you describe Nia's personality?***

Nia (1) enjoys exploring options (openness to experience), (2) believes she is the captain of her own ship (internal locus of control), (3) possesses a positive regard for herself (high self-esteem), (4) likes taking risks (risk taking), and (5) initiates action rather than waits for directions (proactive orientation). These traits are based on the Five Factor Model of personality, which is considered in depth in the Instructor's Resources following chapter five. Her planning facility and comfort with details suggests she is conscientious.

While these traits have undoubtedly contributed to her success in corporate America, others may view her as pushy (low agreeableness), excitable (negative emotionality), and too sure of her own opinions (overconfidence bias). She might also be perceived as Machiavellian, given the way she cleverly responded to Ward's casual remark about curds.

Q2 ***In general terms what is Nia's strategic logic? Is this a sound proposal for Novarum?***

In theory, strategic plans derive from a scan of the environment, looking for social, economic, political, and technical trends that may threaten or provide opportunities for the firm. Potential threats and opportunities are assessed in light of the corporation's strengths and weaknesses, producing plausible scenarios from which the executive team sets specific goals and dedicates significant resources, usually over several years.

Nia's proposal can be defended in general strategic terms as such:

- Novarum must sell its products to the world market; it must become a more global firm. Engaging in a joint venture with a well-regarded local firm is prudent.
- R&D and sales of birth control drugs is problematic in the U.S. because of well-organized religious opposition. Doing research and selling abroad does not stimulate opposition at home.
- Launching a new product in a foreign country is pricey. A joint venture will not be as costly to Novarum as going it alone. Temel Ilac is apparently able to contribute to the cost of research, clinical trials, and marketing.
- All major drug companies need new blockbusters to offset their patent expirations and competition from generics and biosimilars.
- The market is too big to ignore. Islam is the world's largest religion, with over 1 billion people concentrated in 56 predominately Muslim countries stretching from North Africa to the Far East.
- Islamic law permits birth control.
- The competition for a new generation of inexpensive and easy-to-use birth control appears negligible. Novarum can gain first-mover advantage by creating a safe and inexpensive birth control method.

- Moreover, the argument for forming an alliance with Turkey for the pilot project has several good points.
- Turkey is a unique Middle Eastern country: officially secular, yet 98% Muslim, a functioning, albeit immature democracy, NATO member, and a strong candidate for inclusion in the European Union within 10 years. The nation will not do anything to jeopardize its candidacy. It wants to be seen as stable, probusiness and democratic—not as an anticapitalist, religiously reactionary state such as many of its neighbors.
- The vast majority of Turkey's 70 million citizens are Westward leaning. Why? Because of the extraordinary transformational leadership of Mustafa Kemal (often referred to as Ataturk) in the 1920s and 1930s. Ataturk put Turkey, unlike any other country in the Muslim world, on a Western course concerning the importance of education and the scientific method, capitalism, democracy (their constitution is modeled on Switzerland's), nationalism—not Islam—as the shared cultural value for all its citizens, modern dress, separation of church and state, religious tolerance and equal rights for women.
- The Turkish market for family planning is a big, *government-acknowledged* social and economic problem. Rather than creating a need, Novarum will be fulfilling a need in a country whose rapid modernization is creating a large number of dispossessed citizens who have neither the skills nor inclination to join the 21st-century global community.
- Most Turks are not radical Islamists. Rather, most are moderate Muslims who accept Western technology and advocate tolerance for others views. Less than 5% are radical Muslims who seek a return to Sharia law to replace democracy.

See also the *Pharmaceutical Industry Background* and *Opportunities and Threats* sections in this volume.

Q3 *What is the ethical basis of Nia's proposal?*

Of course, an ethical issue can be analyzed from several perspectives, ranging from simple egoism, utilitarianism, relativism, and ending with virtue. At this early point in the story, we might infer that Nia views working with a firm located in an Islamic-oriented nation creates benefits for all stakeholders: herself, Allen, other Novarum employees, Novarum's investors, Temel Ilac, the Turkish economy, and possibly the greater Muslim world. Further, she believes the joint venture may serve as a role model for other Western firms.

And viewed outside the perspective of the company, this particular project might accomplish things that most of the educated world would consider social goods. Namely, it could help to curb population growth, and it could help to empower women by giving them greater control over the disposition of their own bodies.

(*Note*: It is too early to discuss drug pricing. But if Novarum prices the drug fairly, based on each country's ability to pay rather than a fixed price to all customers, one could argue that the cause of social justice will be advanced.)

Q4 *Why is Allen initially opposed to the proposal?*

At this point, it appears that Allen views doing business with Muslims, even Turkish Muslims, as far too risky a proposition. He views the value system of Middle Eastern Muslims as at odds with Western values regarding government, civil society, and business practices. Further, Islamic fundamentalism and ethnocentric behavior is a potentially explosive combination. The Middle East is unstable and unpredictable. Capitalism requires social stability, internationally recognized contract law, minimal corruption, and peaceful resolution of business disputes to flourish.

- Turkey's refusal to officially admit their involvement in the perceived genocide of Armenians in 1915 is another time bomb. The Kurds and Armenians could band together to foment instability on Turkey's Eastern border. Not to mention the U.S. war in Iraq (as of 2009) and the always militant Iran, two other bordering countries with uncertain futures vis-à-vis the West.
- Novarum's birth control drug could be misinterpreted on the volatile "Arab street" as sterilization, in explicit violation of Islamic law.
- The Kurds' separatist movement continues to plague Turkey, and the government's heavy-handed way of stifling legitimate complaints exacerbates the crisis. Human rights abuses, especially of the Kurds, are a prime reason why the EU did not grant Turkey admission during its most recent round of expansion from 15 to 25 countries.
- Allen apparently embraces Huntington's "clash of civilizations" thesis. (see Chapter 6).

Allen worries that Novarum may inadvertently, perhaps circuitously, fund terrorists. His personal loss on September 11 probably shapes his selective perception, stereotypical thinking, and confirmation bias of the proposal. He may, for example, tune into news reports that highlight the tiny percentage of Muslims who are terrorists and disregard the vast majority of Muslims who lead peaceful lives. He appears to be engaging in a form of ethnic profiling, scrutinizing the motives of the Temel Ilac group. Would he have these same reservations about a cross-border joint venture with, say, a Swiss R&D firm?

Q5 ***How might Ward's view of outsourcing and foreign alliances be affected by his experience with his Visa bill?***

The constrained responses of Becky, the call center employee, reflects some of the limitations of scripted systems. Scripted systems have a difficult time dealing with deviations and special cases. Moreover, because the call center personnel are increasingly foreign to the U.S., their ability to deal with more subtle problems is limited by language barriers.

Although she is reading from scripts, Becky may well be operating a type of software known as an expert system. Expert systems are one form of knowledge management (KM). KM is defined as a deliberate attempt to flatten the learning curve by gathering and sharing best practices within the organization, often aided by IT. While a good idea in theory, the practice often yields less-than-hoped-for results, because it is very difficult to gather tacit knowledge from superior performers and reduce it to Web pages, scripts, or memos. Often critical pieces of the process are left out.

In Ward's case, the call center staff member has a formulaic way of responding to problems. But her questions and comments are not quite on point, and they become increasingly exasperating to Ward, who is caught up in the "heavy machinery" of an efficient, but nonresponsive system.

Ward's situation is humorous, in part, because the stakes are so small. Ward can extrapolate from his experience with a trivial credit card charge, however, to the potential disastrous results of miscommunication across nations when manufacturing drugs for human consumption. Hence, his reversal on the Novarum collaboration with Temel Ilac. But we may be giving Ward too much credit in this analysis. His picturing of Becky in a sari and wondering whether the management canes its employees shows cultural and racial stereotyping and bias. He may be against the project just out of prejudice.

Rational systems have their uses, most notably when dealing with routine procedures. Ironically, in the extreme, rational systems can become irrational because they lack creativity. Rational systems are predictable, calculable, and efficient—the assembly line being the exemplar. In a postindustrial world, rational systems, and, yes, assembly lines will have a place, but they will always have limits.

Q6 *Which leadership and organizational behavior theories provide insight into Allen's reaction to his call from a board member?*

Allen controls his emotions in response to Eleanor's directive that Novarum adopt a more international approach to doing business. He likely feels that Eleanor's direction is not strategically smart, yet he displays no anger or disappointment. Rather, he immediately agrees with her. His ability to remain calm—emotional adjustment—is a source of strength for any leader, but especially for CEOs, who are under constant pressure and scrutiny from multiple stakeholders.

His chameleon-like behavior is a form of self-monitoring, whereby he is conscious of the impact he has on others. In this case he wants to present himself to his boss as cooperative. Most CEOs are politically adept, contributing mightily to their rise in the corporate hierarchy. Allen is no exception.

Allen is emotionally upset by Eleanor's phone call. His mood has darkened, and he likely intends to speak with Nia about corporate protocol.

Human trust depends on integrity. Allen feels betrayed by Nia. She breached his trust by violating a well-established norm of honoring the chain of command. Nia argued her case to her boss's boss without his permission.

Q7 *What other theories help you to understand the behavior of Eleanor, Allen, and Nia?*

Eleanor is not completely truthful with Allen; Allen lies to Eleanor, a fact she is aware of. The lack of honesty may diminish the view they hold of each other, perhaps unconsciously.

Nia uses the power tactic of coalition building with Eleanor to further her agenda.

All three executives possess an internal locus of control, and are capable of rationalizations to justify Machiavellian behavior.

Given the ease with which the three executives withhold information from each other to meet their goals, we might describe the culture as political in a pejorative sense.

2

Strategic Planning and Affliction

Nia accepted an invitation to do Career Day from the principal of Cady Stanton High School, who was also her neighbor across the street in Partridgeberry Meadows. Nia had bought a McMansion in Partridgeberry Meadows shortly after she came to work for Novarum Pharmaceuticals. She didn't feel like a person who would live in a place called Partridgeberry Meadows, and once she got to know her neighbors, she didn't think they were, either. She thought it interesting that such a pretentiously named development could harbor such down-to-earth people. This led her to formulate a sort of law for living: never judge people by the name of their housing development.

Career Day featured nearly a dozen 10-minute presentations, but Nia was the only one who brought a laptop. The man who was on stage before her, a fireman from Gary, wore firefighting getup. He was about 10 years younger than Nia. He had a ruddy color and a day's growth of beard and he spoke knowledgeably to the students about "knocking down" fires. Like a general giving a briefing on the activities of the enemy, he spoke of a fire as "he." In spite of herself, Nia thought the fireman was sexy.

The Varieties of Leadership at Novarum Pharmaceuticals: A Novel, pages 27–48

The fireman turned his presentation into a firefighting demonstration. He had brought along a wooden door in a frame that was set up on stage. He talked about the problem that a locked door presents to a firefighter, then he donned his helmet, lowered a clear visor over his eyes, and completely splintered the door in three well-placed strokes of a large axe. The students cheered.

The firefighter took off his helmet. He didn't bow. He didn't even smile. He stood among the splinters and chunks of wood that littered the stage with the axe upended beside him. "Are there any questions?"

A student in the front row stood up. "How much money do you make?"

It was, as the standup comedians say, a tough room.

The firefighter looked flustered. He mumbled something that seemed to include the phrase "union scale," but Nia didn't catch the rest of it. She realized she had better put together some sort of reply to that question. She would have to say something evasive. Even if she didn't feel that it was none of their business, she wouldn't have wanted to talk about it. She had found out 3 weeks ago that Ward Alexander made 35% more than she did with essentially the same levels of responsibility and experience. She couldn't do a thing about it without putting Jenna, her buddy in Human Resources, at risk. Pay equity is an odd thing, she thought. Prior to discovering Ward's salary, she was quite satisfied with her six-figure income. So judgments about compensation were absolute and relative. Still, she had been suffering her pay inequity in silence ever since finding out. Eleanor had counseled her to channel her anger and bide her time. Where would she be without Eleanor?

When Nia's turn came, she put up her first PowerPoint slide, which was a definition of strategic planning:

> Strategic planning is an intuitive and disciplined process of overlapping and iterative plans and actions to move the entire organization—or major business unit—in a new direction over a few years. Business strategy seeks to align the organization's (or business unit's) behavior more closely to its customers' needs, wants, and potentialities.

She read out the definition as dramatically as she could, then looked around to see if they were getting it. The students seemed to be talking in little clumps throughout the auditorium. Here and there, a few appeared to be asleep. A couple in the back row was making out. She might as well be presenting this to an empty auditorium for all they were getting out of it.

How do you give a presentation to an audience that doesn't want to be there in the first place and probably doesn't believe a word you say in the second? Maybe something a little more interactive.

With a certain amount of trepidation, she stepped away from the podium and walked back and forth across the stage, kicking aside bits of wood left from the fireman's demonstration. "What's your favorite band?" she called out.

The couple that was making out paid no attention to her, but most of the rest looked up at her from their conversations, texting, or naps.

"Eminem," shouted someone.

"I said 'band,'" said Nia. "Isn't that a candy?"

A few students laughed, but more jeered.

"OK," said Nia. "I'm not up to date on music. But you tell me. What's your favorite band?"

"Coldplay," someone shouted.

Before Nia could answer, someone shouted "Audioslave." And then the names came faster, the students throwing them at her, as if they might overwhelm her. Death Cab for Cutie. Snow Patrol. Ak-Momo. Iron and Wine. She recognized none of the names, but in the midst of the confusion, one phrase caught her attention. She held up a hand to stop them. "Who said Cowboy Junkies?" she said.

"I did." The voice belonged to a girl with black lipstick and dark hair artfully arranged in clumps, although Nia could not have identified what artform informed the arrangement.

"Let's go with Cowboy Junkies." She looked around the room. "Who can tell me the mission of Cowboy Junkies?"

They looked at her with curiosity, but it was plain she had their attention.

"Whatever else it is," said Nia, "Cowboy Junkies is a business. You can't have a business without a strategic plan. This morning, we're going to formulate a strategic plan for Cowboy Junkies. To do that, we have to start with their mission statement. If you were the Cowboy Junkies, what would you say you were trying to do in the music business?"

They continued to look at her with questions but no answers.

"What do the Cowboy Junkies do that makes them distinctive, and what are they trying to accomplish in the marketplace?"

Many of the students squirmed, as if embarrassed at not knowing.

"OK. What kind of music do the Cowboy Junkies play?"

The girl with the black lipstick explained. "Alternative country surreal rock."

"Are they the best alternative country surreal rock band out there?"

The girl didn't answer but looked at Nia as if she'd just arrived from Jupiter and perhaps could be forgiven her bottomless ignorance of music. She could see some of the other audience members beginning to lean forward in their seats.

"Now we're getting somewhere," said Nia. "If I were running the Cowboy Junkies, I would probably write a mission statement that said something like, 'Our goal is to make money by entertaining fans of alternative country surreal rock music with excellent recordings and concerts. We make our music available to our fans on CD and online and through live concerts.'"

By this time, she had everyone's attention, with the exception of the make-out artists in the back row. "Now I'm going to show you the steps you go through to build a strategic plan from this mission statement so the Cowboy Junkies will have some idea of where they're going for the next five years."

As she paced back and forth, she fired questions at them. The students began vying to answer. Some of them shouted. Nia soon stopped pacing and returned to the podium, quit PowerPoint, and opened a word processing document, so she could record notes that the students could see on the screen behind her. She chose a large, bold font and began typing in the answers to her step-by-step questions as the students provided them. There were a few missteps, but Nia kept them focused on the highlights. It took about 10 minutes to get through the process. She could see she was running over her allotted time, but the principal signaled her to keep going. Even the fireman, who had taken a seat in the front row, was engrossed.

It was the kind of stuff she wished she'd been doing at Novarum Pharmaceuticals for the past 2 years. It's amazing how much brainpower there is in a collection of interested human beings, even high school students. When they were finished, they had a one-page strategic plan for the Cowboy Junkies.

"There you have it. That's strategic planning." Nia looked around and paused for effect. "I guarantee that the Cowboy Junkies are using a plan that is something like this one. They have to. They're a business. And if you don't know where the business is going, how will you know when you get there?"

To her gratified surprise, they applauded. Nia felt even higher than she'd felt after a particularly successful presentation at the annual meeting of the Strategic Planning Society last year.

Once the students had all filed out and the principal had thanked all the presenters, Nia gathered up her laptop and her purse and wandered out into the bright corridor of the school building. She switched on her cell phone and saw there was a message from Eleanor. She called in to retrieve it. While she was waiting for the call to connect, she saw a group of three girls standing some distance down the hall. They were looking at her, and she smiled at them.

Eleanor's message was long, but they tended to leave long phone messages in the Old Girls Network. They trusted nothing to e-mail.

"Hi, Nia. I wanted to let you know that I called Allen and talked with him about the Turkish project." She laughed. "I made him an offer he can't refuse. You see, he can't go against a plan with the support of a majority of the Board. But he really seemed to be fine with it. He was willing to let me think he had never cancelled the Temel Ilac project to begin with and even seemed anxious to take credit for it. From our last conversation about it, I thought you wouldn't object to that, since the project is so much more important than who gets credit for it. Let him continue to believe it's his baby and you'll have both Turkey and the support of your CEO. Good luck. Bye."

This was very good news. Nia generally resisted the temptation to care about something as petty as who gets the credit. What she cared about was dragging Novarum Pharmaceuticals into the era of globalization and doing it in a way that made it an ally of the women of Turkey. She felt excited, and she wanted to call Eleanor back, but one of the girls detached herself from the group down the hallway and approached her. Nia recognized her as the girl with the black lipstick. The girl's two companions stood about 20 feet away, as if waiting to reinforce her should this sortie fail.

"Ms. Stevens." The student held out her hand. Her voice was polite and respectful, even if her appearance was outlandish almost to the point of offensiveness. She wore a tee shirt with strange symbols on it: a man with a goat's head, five-pointed stars, and a number of graphics Nia didn't recognize. She wondered if the symbols were satanic. A tattoo that looked like blue barbed wire encircled the girl's pale upper arm. There was a small jeweled stud in the side of her left nostril. "My name is Affliction."

Nia took the hand offered her. "Affliction? Really?"

"I changed it," said the girl. "The change isn't legal yet, but it will be as soon as I'm twenty-one."

Nia nodded.

"I just wanted to tell you how much I liked your presentation."

"Thank you," said Nia.

"I'm very interested in strategic planning."

Nia wanted to tell her that she'd never get through the front door of about 498 of the Fortune 500 companies unless she started grooming herself better. But why start that argument here? The girl's appearance seemed a deliberate provocation. Nia tried not to feel provoked. After all, if she should not judge people by the name of their housing developments, how could she judge a young woman by the color of her lipstick? She imagined Affliction working in her office. It would be like diversity management with a vengeance. But isn't that what management's all about?

"I wanted to ask you," Affliction said, "if you could give me the mission statement for Novarum Pharmaceuticals."

So the girl had gotten the lesson. Nia felt a pleasant warmth rise from her abdomen into her chest. "I'll do better than that," she said. "I'll tell you where to find it. Visit our Web site: www.novarumpharma.com."

"Why is that better?"

"Because looking for it will give you practice with an important research tool. About ninety percent of American companies put their mission statements on their Web sites."

Affliction smiled in a way that made her look like the schoolgirl she was rather than a denizen of a B-grade horror movie. "I'll check it out," she said. "Did you write it?"

"No," said Nia. "But I like to think they hired me to make sure it was realized."

Affliction seemed impressed by this answer. "Ms. Stevens," she said, "is there any possibility I might meet you at your office one day, just to see what it's like?"

Her enthusiasm was touching. That would probably last until she saw how things really were in the corporate world: when she discovered, for example, that a male executive in the same company doing comparable work, earned plenty more.

She looked at Affliction, wondering if she might mentor this girl. The first thing she would do is speak with her forthrightly about protective coloration and how important it could be in business. Outside the music industry, business people don't wear black lipstick or arrange their hair in clumps. It distracts people from the business at hand. She reached into her purse and retrieved one of her business cards. She handed it to Affliction. "Call me during the day sometime and we'll set something up."

"Oh, this is frigid!" said Affliction.

The word itself didn't sound positive, but her voice was infused with delight. The slang would have to go too.

Affliction rejoined her companions and they giggled together the way high school girls have been doing as long as there have been high schools and girls.

Nia walked out into the sunlight. Her German sports car stood out like a spot of fresh hollandaise on a platter of graying, overcooked vegetables. She set off toward it with a spring in her step. The Turkish project was on.

She was still surfing the excitement of getting her project approved, and she wanted to call Eleanor back to celebrate, but she thought it might be better for her to seem a little cooler about it. In any case, she decided not to call Eleanor until Allen told her himself about his reversal and she had something more to report.

At the office, she asked her assistant, Jack, for an update.

"Allen has asked you to come see him as soon as you got in," he said.

"Is there anything here that needs attention right now?"

"Nothing as important as Allen," he said.

That was one of the things she liked about Jack. He knew how to prioritize her work life. He knew that the first duty in his job description was to keep her happy, in the same way he knew that the first duty in her job description was to keep Allen happy.

She dropped her laptop and purse on her desk, then set off down the quiet corridor toward Allen's corner office. She walked slowly in order to try to contain her excitement. Allen's assistant sent her right in.

Allen looked up and smiled that winning smile of his. "Nia." He took her hand as if he hadn't seen her for several months. He gestured at the chair across from his desk.

"I'm sorry I wasn't in when you called, Allen." She sat in the chair. "I was doing a high school Career Day."

"How did it go?"

"I didn't expect much interest since I went on after the fireman." Nia paused. "He brought an axe."

Allen laughed. "You didn't bring an axe?"

"I brought PowerPoint."

Allen laughed heartily at this and the two of them laughed together for a moment, and it made Nia feel closer to Allen than she'd felt before. Then Allen got his breath and spoke again.

"Maybe a knife would have been more appropriate." He was no longer smiling.

It sounded like a joke, but Allen's eyes had suddenly become hard. Nia stopped laughing. The room felt as if the shadow of a giant raptor had passed over. "I don't understand."

"I got a call from Eleanor Marcus late yesterday." Allen leaned forward in his chair. "But I imagine you already know that, don't you?"

Nia could feel self-doubt pooling in her abdomen. She knew about the call. Yet she remained silent. It was strange to feel shame when she had done nothing wrong.

"I understand now why she recommended you for this job," he said.

The attack hit her where she lived. Nia found her voice. "I do well in this job."

"Yes, you do," said Allen. "But I don't like having Eleanor Marcus's dogsbody in my office. I feel like I'm being spied on."

Nia had never heard the word "dogsbody" before, but she gathered from the context that it meant something like stooge. He was coming down on her for telling Eleanor about the Turkish project's cancellation.

"Are we supposed to keep our work secret from the Board of Directors, Allen?"

That took away Allen's momentum. He sat back in his chair. "No, of course not."

"Then why is there a problem?" said Nia. "I felt my project wasn't getting the chance it deserved, and I took my concerns to my mentor, in the same way I speak with her about my career in general and have for several years."

"That project took the time of three top-level executives. It got a fair chance."

"I think that's exactly the issue, Allen."

He looked at her blankly. "What do you mean?"

"Fairness is the issue. My project didn't get a fair chance, and I'm not being treated fairly right now."

"What are you talking about?"

"I conceived of and fought for a project with enormous profit potential and did what needed to be done to make it happen. If I were a man, you'd be giving me fifty-yard line tickets to Soldier Field."

"Don't tell me you can't see anything wrong with going over my head. You're smarter than that."

Nia noticed he ignored her main point and realized he was sensitive to it. So she focused on it. "We wouldn't be having this discussion if I were a man," she said.

Allen made a dismissive gesture. "That's absurd!"

"This is the first real strategic project I've worked on since I got here," she said, "and you've given me no support on it. I've had to put this thing together entirely on my own, and I've had to squeeze the time out from a lot of other responsibilities you've piled on me. You've overloaded me with product rollouts, investor relations, and media opportunities. I'm not a strategic planner, I'm a staff functionary, Allen! "

"You're changing the subject," said Allen.

"I'm addressing the only subject that's relevant."

"It has nothing to do with anything, and it's not true."

Nia realized it was time to play her trump card. She had to bring up her salary, but she had to do it in a way that wouldn't implicate her source. Then she decided on her line of attack. She would ask him point blank.

"If it's not true," said Nia, "tell me this. Do I get the same salary as any male executive doing an equivalent job?"

Allen didn't even bat an eye. "Yes."

* * *

On Wednesday, Jenna's assistant brought her a problem with the new human resources management system. The software wouldn't accept one of the entries for the Marketing Department's level-two admins. The message said, "Error 2519."

There was of course no manual to explain what error 2519 might be, and Jenna hesitated to call Information Technology, because she knew from experience some of the staff were hard to work with unless you told them it was an emergency. And if you used the emergency gambit too many times, they stopped answering your requests altogether. Jenna had no idea what constituted too many times, but she didn't want to find out either. She prided herself on never yet having called IT with an emergency about the human resources management system.

Jenna had been with Novarum Pharmaceuticals for 8 years, and the first she'd known of the new human resources management system, which everybody called the HRIS, was when Ward hired Frank Maldonado to replace Wendy, who had recently retired as the Director of Human Resources. Frank had been Jenna's boss for 6 months now, notwithstanding he was several years younger than she was. But he was experienced with the enterprise software, which the company had bought from a German firm famous for installing it through the length and breadth of the business world.

Fortunately, this error 2519 thing was the kind of problem Jenna loved. Months of working with the HRIS gave her an appreciation of it and she felt more at home with it than most Novarum Pharmaceuticals. Of course, most Novarum Pharmaceuticals employees resented the system, because during the transition to it from the old one, they had to maintain two different systems at once. They regarded the HRIS more an intruder than an improvement over the old "system," which was not a system at all but a series of overlapping processes and patches—a database for time records, a paper form for employee reclassifications, a handbook in a loose-leaf binder, and so on—that had grown like dirty laundry in a hamper.

However complicated, Jenna could lose herself completely in the HRIS, going from screen to screen looking for some pattern that would reveal its reasoning in accepting an entry for one employee while denying it for another.

She started by comparing Marketing to Operations, which also had two level-two admins. The system had not rejected any entries for Operations. And the situation was very similar. But she knew that her mind was a generalizing machine, which meant that she tended to see how things were alike with very little effort. The German software, on the other hand, was a particularizing machine. It was in the business of looking for differences.

She stared at the screen for a while, waiting for inspiration. None came, so she jotted down the employee numbers for each of the four level-two admins, the two from Operations and the two from Marketing. Then she brought up the employee profile request screen and entered the employee numbers one by one. Soon she had four employee profiles, which she tiled on the screen so she could look at all of them at the same time.

All four of the admins were women, so it couldn't be gender. They were all level two, so it couldn't be a level problem. Three of them had incept dates in the range of 5 to 10 years. The remaining one had an incept date of 11 years. She went to the file cabinet and retrieved the loose-leaf policy manual to look up the profit-sharing vesting policy. Vesting had only the most tenuous connection to the question, but Jenna had often found in the past that the system operated in ways that were very obscure.

She was running her finger down the page, trying to find the subheading on vesting, when she was aware of someone standing in front of her desk. She held her finger on the page and looked up. It was Frank. He was smiling that I've-got-bad-news-please-don't-hate-me smile of his. Jenna could not say she was happy to see Maldonado. He wasn't a very good boss. While he clearly knew a lot about the HRIS, there was something about him that made him difficult to trust. He was a shirtsleeves kind of guy, yet he wore the shirtsleeves rolled up to a precise point half-way up his forearms, and Jenna often wondered if he didn't do it just to make his Rolex more visible.

She realized it was Wednesday afternoon. Frank always appeared at her desk Wednesday afternoon.

"I'm sorry to interrupt you, Jenna."

Jenna said nothing. Frank was always polite in an aloof sort of way that made one further doubt his trustworthiness. Most managers wouldn't apologize like that. But after all, you don't have to apologize unless you do something bad or unpleasant.

"Well then," he said. "I just wanted to tell you that Ward gave me the word. You may have to work this weekend. I thought it might be helpful if I gave you some notice."

Jenna almost winced when he said Ward's name. She found it difficult to trust someone who blamed an order on his boss rather than taking responsibility for it.

"OK," said Jenna.

He waited for a moment, smiling at her, but she said nothing else, so he finally turned and left.

If he thought she was going to thank him for this "advanced notice," he had another thing coming. Of course it was helpful to get some notice, but he'd been coming to her on Wednesdays with the same message for the past 2 months. She'd had to work one of those weeks, but on all the others, he came by late on Friday to tell her she wasn't going to have to work after all.

To be sure, she had always felt relieved at not having to work, but the third time it happened, she realized he had managed to appropriate her weekends. If you can't plan for your weekend, you don't even own it. Yet here was Maldonado, acting like the seven out of eight weekends she didn't have to work were some kind of company benefit.

She looked down. Her finger rested next to a subhead half-way down a page of the manual, but she couldn't remember what she was looking up now.

She looked back at her computer screen. The employee records had been displaced by a colorful fireworks display. She reached over and tapped a key to restore the screen she'd been looking at. The fireworks vanished and the four employee records reappeared. And then she saw why the system had refused the record of the fourth employee. She'd been at Novarum Pharmaceuticals the longest, and she also had the highest salary. It was so high, in fact, it exceeded the limit for a level-two admin. She was, in other words, just the kind of case the HRIS was designed to eliminate.

Jenna changed the employee's salary level classification to "miscellaneous," went back to the Marketing Department's listing screen, and entered her number. The system accepted the entry gracefully.

She swelled with pride. How many people at Novarum could actually outwit The System? She started to telephone her sister to tell her she couldn't go canoeing this weekend after all when she stopped herself. There was a seven in eight chance she *could go*, and those were pretty good odds.

* * *

Reynold played handball with Allen three evenings a week. He was Allen's family physician and had been, more or less, since they'd shared an ortho round during residency. The handball started 2 years ago when Reynold had treated Allen for chest pains. An EKG and a physical examination convinced Reynold it was gas. He talked with Allen about his job and eventually figured out that stress made him eat too fast, and eating too fast gave him gas. It sometimes seemed to Reynold that the increasing complexities of life tended to simplify health problems. You eat too fast, you get gas. You get gas, you have chest pains.

So Reynold had prescribed a treatment commensurate with the problem: slower eating. And, since Reynold's specialty was sports medicine—Allen was one of only a handful of general practice patients he saw—he also prescribed an exercise bike.

"It's time for you to think seriously about your cardiovascular health anyway," he'd said to Allen.

But Allen had called him after a week, complaining the exercise bike was the most tedious activity he'd ever engaged in. He said he had been involved in hostile takeovers that were more fun.

So Reynold prescribed handball with his family doctor. That worked out just fine, because Allen was a ferocious competitor and the games helped Reynold keep up his handball skills. Within a month of playing regularly, they were evenly matched. At the same skill level, Allen won most games—as the result of sheer drive. It worked out fine, though, because although Allen seemed to be prepared to do anything to win, he was gracious in victory and his company was always pleasant.

But Allen showed up for this particular session in a black mood. He spoke little and he played furiously. Having won the coin toss, he served first. He ran five successful rallies very rapidly, mostly because of the force with which he hit the ball.

Five points down, Reynold finally managed to gain the serve, but Allen recovered it on the first rally. He then ran another three points. He had ten points before Reynold scored one, which was unusual. In the end, he took the game, 21 to 12. He made the 21st point on a wrist ball, but he apparently thought Reynold didn't notice.

The rest of the games were much like the first, with Allen driving hard and moving so fast he didn't stop play for faults. Reynold found the spectacle too engrossing to call attention to them.

Reynold liked cooling down in the juice bar after a game almost as much as he liked the activity of the game itself. He liked listening to Allen talk about the problems of running a large corporation. It was as different from Reynold's experience of running a small practice as it could possibly be.

The two tired, sweating men sat at a small table and sipped iced mineral water from plastic cups.

"You played pretty hard today," said Reynold.

"It was a tough day at work," said Allen. "I had some steam to blow off."

"Anything you can talk about?" said Reynold.

Allen looked at him for a moment. He finally took a sip of his water. "You have people reporting to you, right?"

Reynold nodded and waited for him to continue.

"Do you ever feel like you're being managed by them?"

"Of course," said Reynold. "I thought every manager felt that way."

"I didn't," said Allen, "at least until today."

"What happened today?"

"I have an insubordinate executive—"

Reynold stopped him. "Give me the particulars. What constitutes insubordination?"

"In this case, she went over my head to the Board of Directors, and she and a director with whom she's close engineered a scheme to make me approve a project I had already rejected."

"You said she was managing you," said Reynold. "That sounds less like management than deviousness."

"I didn't tell you about the bad part yet."

"Oh, continue then."

"Today, she tried to trap me into telling her that she's paid less than a male executive with equivalent responsibilities."

"How did you get out of that?"

"I told her she's paid the same."

"Is she?"

"No. She gets thirty-five percent less."

Reynold took a swallow from his cup and caught an ice cube. He took a moment to crunch on it before speaking. "Let me see if I have the essentials here. She asked you if she was paid on the same scale as the other executives, and you told a lie and said she was."

"I wouldn't exactly call it a lie," said Allen.

Reynold shook another ice cube out of his now drained cup. He squinted with one eye as he shattered the cube between his molars.

"What, exactly, would you call it?"

"You don't understand," said Allen. "Salaries are very personal matters, and they are highly confidential. You can't tell one employee what another employee makes. You can't even hint at it."

"So you preserve this confidentiality by lying?"

"That's not the point," said Allen.

"Oh?"

"The point," said Allen, "is that she went over my head, and when I called her on the carpet for it, she somehow manipulated the conversation into a gender equity thing, and then she asked me if she was paid the same as the others."

"And that's when you lied to her about it," said Reynold.

"You don't understand," Allen repeated. "I had to keep her from finding out because she was claiming it was a gender equity thing. Do you have any idea how much trouble that can cause?"

Reynold was beginning to find this amusing. "So you had to keep from confirming the gender inequity that she only suspected."

"There's no gender inequity," said Allen.

"I thought you just told me she's paid thirty-five percent less than the guy who's at her level."

"Yes, but not because of gender."

"Why, then?"

"The labor market," said Allen. "I don't pay her thirty-five percent less because she's a woman. I pay her thirty-five percent less because I can. If she'll take thirty-five percent less, I'd be a fool to pay her more."

"Why do you think she is willing to take thirty-five percent less?" said Reynold.

Allen shrugged. "She's a woman. That's what women get paid. I can't pay her more. I have a duty to the stockholders."

Reynold laughed. "Heaven protect us from those who have a duty to the stockholders, for they are legion, and they screw us all royally in pursuit of that duty."

Allen got a look on his face—part disappointment, part anger—that Reynold had never seen before. It was a little scary.

Reynold stopped laughing. "I'm sorry, Allen. That was uncalled-for. I shouldn't have been so cavalier." He shrugged. "It's just that for a moment, you sounded a little like somebody from one of the third-party insurance companies, and I got carried away. I'm sorry."

Allen seemed to relax a little, but he remained watchful and silent.

"You know," said Reynold, "I could never understand why you left U. Rochester Hospital for this corporate thing. You could be a successful clinician if you wanted to, and I think you'd be happier."

It was an old contention between them, but it had always been good-natured, and Reynold sensed now that it was better to get back to something they shared, even a disagreement, rather than continue on toward the feelings he'd glimpsed in Allen's face.

"That's right," said Allen, with residual irritation, "you don't understand."

Reynold thought he should try again. "Let's start over. Why did you reject this woman's project in the first place? Were the numbers out of line?"

"No," said Allen. "The numbers were good. But when I make a decision like that, I have to look at more than numbers." He sipped the last of his mineral water. "I don't think it's a wise idea to form an alliance with a Muslim company, and especially not one in Turkey, where they're having a resurgence of fundamentalism."

"I don't know much about it," said Reynold, "but I thought Turkey was a secular country. Ataturk and all that."

"It has a secular constitution and it has outlawed political parties based on religion, but like every other place in the Islamic world, it's having trouble controlling the fanatics who want the country to live under Sharia."

"Why does she want this project?"

"She has a lot of good business reasons," said Allen. "But frankly, I think her strongest motivation is to save the women of Turkey from these fundamentalists."

"How does the project do that?"

"We have sketched out the requirements for a new birth control preparation." Allen ticked off the characteristics on the fingers of one hand. "More than ninety-nine percent effective. Minimal side effects. Foolproof delivery that can be kept secret from a woman's family."

"Sounds to me like you're describing implants," said Reynold.

Allen shook his head. "You can see implants on the surface of the skin. In the developing world, husbands have been known to cut out their wives' implants."

Reynold gave a little shiver. "They must really want kids."

Allen dismissed the opinion. "That hardly matters. In a lot of countries, there is nothing more important than a husband's authority over his wife. Birth control undermines it. If women can't control when they are going to be pregnant, they can't control any aspect of their lives."

"And you're against that?"

"Not at all," said Allen. "I want to develop this product. I just don't want to send American jobs to Turkey to do it, especially not with a company that there's no way to really know whether they have terrorist associations."

"And yet, this woman has put together a deal that looks good on paper and has the support of your Board of Directors."

Allen just nodded.

The whole situation was laid out now, and the two men sat silently for a moment. Finally Reynold spoke.

"Do you want my perspective on this?"

"Yes, of course," said Allen. "I'm stuck with it now, but I'd like to hear what you have to say."

Reynold looked him in the eye, a slight smile playing on his lips. "Do what you think is right, but if you win this one on a wrist ball, own up to it."

Instructor's Resources

Learning Goals

Based on reading this chapter and knowledge of leadership and organizational behavior theory, students will be able to

- discuss the concept of equity theory and the consequences of perceived inequity
- explore the concept of equal pay for work of equal value, and difficulties in measuring comparable worth, especially across gender lines
- evaluate the claims on overtime work that an organization can impose on its workers.

Discussion Questions and Possible Instructor's Responses

Q1 *From Nia's standpoint, is her compensation equitable to others?*

Having discovered that Ward's salary is considerably higher than hers, Nia undoubtedly believes her compensation is unfair. Equity theory supplies an explanation for her reasoning. As is often the case, Nia compares her compensation with that of an organizational peer because she has a good idea of his responsibilities and accomplishments. She perceives herself as trumping Ward in several ways: formal education, prior corporate experience, basic competency, and with the Temel Ilac deal, impact on Novarum's future. Other disinterested observers might disagree with her assessment. Classification and compensation specialists have a hard time measuring comparable worth; it is more art than science, more subjective than objective.

Q2 *Which theories can help to predict how Nia will react to learning of Ward's compensation vis-à-vis her own?*

While she is disappointed and angry, expectancy theory predicts Nia will continue to push hard for the strategic alliance with Temel Ilac. Three reasons suggest why: (1) belief in the project's importance, (2) conviction she has the ability to succeed, and (3) probable payoff. Her intrinsic motivation derives from a commitment to liberate women. She also calculates that conceiving a strategically significant project will yield extrinsic rewards. And, if her eventual extrinsic rewards from Novarum (e.g., bonus and promotion) are insufficient to match her efforts on the project, she will use the experience when negotiating with her next employer. Further, Nia's personality, (i.e., internal locus of control and high conscientiousness) makes it likely that she would challenge Allen about her compensation. Hence, equity theory is useful in predicting her behavior.

It is interesting to note the power of equity theory. Prior to discovering the difference between her salary and Ward's, Nia gives no indication that she is dissatisfied with her job or pay. This suggests that compensation—past a threshold—is at least partially a relative concept that satisfies higher-order needs for esteem and status.

Q3 *What reasoning does Allen use in his conversation with Reynold about Nia's compensation, and is it defensible?*

Ironically, Allen also invokes equity theory. But he arrives at the opposite conclusion from Nia to explain the fairness of her compensation. Allen compares Nia with other *females* doing similar jobs, not Ward. Using this benchmark, her compensation is in line with other strategic planning executives. He also implicitly uses the free-market argument. That is, Nia accepted her position without coercion, and she may exit the corporation at any time. Because she accepted the compensation package, she is, ipso facto, fairly compensated. Finally, Allen justifies his position by arguing that he is primarily beholden to the shareholders and therefore should not spend money unnecessarily. We may think Allen is a hypocrite or a fool, but it's important to remember that people are almost never hypocrites or fools in their own minds. Understanding that is vital to managing them.

Q4 ***Is Allen justified in his response to Nia's pointed question about her compensation?***

Allen appears to believe he is justified, and he takes offense at Reynold's suggestion that he is rationalizing. He probably doesn't accept the premise of Nia's question. That is, she wants to be compared with Ward and others at a similar hierarchical level. As noted above, he compares Nia with females in similar roles in other corporations. Further, he certainly shouldn't disclose confidential information about one employee to another. Allen might also argue that the role of strategic planner is not as complex, or has as much accountability requirements as that of CFO, especially in a Sarbanes-Oxley environment.

Q5 ***Is Frank Maldonado an effective manager?***

The little we do know about Frank suggests he does not display interpersonal competency. Jenna doesn't find him trustworthy. He may also lack analytical competencies such as planning, problem solving and resource usage because he apparently isn't able to manage the workflow demands within a normal 40-hour workweek. Habitual, forced overtime work is an indication that a department is not well organized. As a director, Frank's job is, at least in part, to provide higher-ups with a plan to manage the work and to inform executives about the negative consequences of continually mandating professional staff to work overtime. Increased errors, irritability, health problems, reduced customer satisfaction, and unwanted turnover are likely results. Jenna appears to be a technically competent employee. Part of Frank's job is to clear the path for performers such as Jenna, doing everything possible to reduce hindrance stress from their jobs. Leaders display a caring ethic that inspires high performance and morale; managers use position power to gain compliance of subordinates. Frank appears to be relying on the latter because he lacks the former.

Q6 ***Who, if either, has the better case for being angry with the other, Allen or Nia?***

Allen can cite the well-established norm of not violating the chain of command; one does not go around one's boss without permission. However, Allen knows Eleanor is Nia's mentor, so it shouldn't come as too big a surprise to find that Eleanor would advocate for her. Still, Eleanor makes no mention of the origin of "her" strategic alliance idea. But, since she is a Board member, we can conclude that she is in support of the idea, so its origin may be beside the point.

The allegation of sexism is serious. Its truthfulness is hard to discern at this point in the story. Certainly Allen doesn't view himself as a sexist. He views the chain of command as an inviolate management principle, equally applicable to females and males. Her compensation complaint is—to him—baseless. Allen likely feels betrayed by Nia's behavior and subsequent confrontation.

Nia, of course sees it differently. Allen's not telling the truth about her pay. The Temel Ilac alliance is a wise strategic move. Rather than sanction, Allen should applaud her skill in pulling the proposal together and her creativity in overcoming obstacles. The fact that a key Board member was willing to champion the concept speaks to its merits.

Allen and Nia's personalities would tend to heighten the tension. We can infer they both tend toward confrontation rather than agreeableness. We know attitudes and behavior are linked. The "strain toward consistency" moves us to reconcile our acts and attitudes. Nia and Allen acted in ways that might be causing some cognitive dissonance. Of course, the past can't be changed, so we could predict attitudes will harden in support of their opposing behavior. Hence, their advancement of "competing truths" is likely to be heated.

3

Feels So Good

Nia sipped her latte vente. It was hot and rich, and life was good.

"What are you smiling at?" Eleanor set her Frappuccino on the table and sat down across from her.

Nia hadn't realized she was smiling, but now—as Eleanor called her attention to it—she could feel the pleasant fatigue in her cheeks. She had probably been smiling all morning, and on a Monday!

For a year now, Nia had been meeting Eleanor on Monday morning before work. This Starbuck's was halfway between Nia's office in Evanston and Eleanor's office in Chicago, so it had all the usual Starbuck's qualities to recommend it, but it was also away from colleagues and co-workers who might recognize them, and they didn't have to worry about keeping their voices down when speaking of matters that should be confidential to the Old Girls Network.

Nia had been looking forward to this meeting all weekend. She needed Eleanor's advice on handling Allen, but she also wanted to share with her the continuing success of the Turkey project. She had spoken to Rasheed at

The Varieties of Leadership at Novarum Pharmaceuticals: A Novel, pages 49–64

the end of last week, and he'd reported that everything was now in place for data sharing between Temel Ilac and Novarum Pharmaceuticals. To Nia's way of thinking, it was the most delicate step in the project—the careful courtship ritual between two companies that have agreed to the intimacy of a shared database. If Novarum Pharmaceuticals and Temel Ilac had been people rather than corporations, this would have been the date on which they both knew they were going to have sex.

"I'm smiling at the success of the Old Girls Network," said Nia.

Eleanor nodded and sipped her coffee. "Mmmm. Good." She put the cup down. "I think Starbuck's owes at least part of its success to a principle that nobody ever expresses openly."

Nia leaned forward to catch whatever was coming next. Smooth jazz murmured soothingly from a speaker overhead. Eleanor's little lectures, which were always insightful, were one of the things Nia liked best about their relationship. "What principle is that?"

"Few of us can have the best of everything, but almost everyone can have the best of something." Eleanor's classically cut, stainless-steel colored hair shone in the morning light from the window. She sipped again from her Frappuccino. "Even if you drive a Hyundai and live in a packing crate, you can still pony up $4.75 for a steaming Frappuccino and know you're getting a coffee that's as good as what Bill Gates drinks."

"Bill Gates?"

"Are you taking issue with my choice of symbols?"

"You could have said Melinda Gates."

"I could have said Oprah or the Queen of England, for that matter. What are we arguing about?"

"I'm not arguing," said Nia.

"You're giving a convincing imitation of someone who is."

"Because you're giving a convincing imitation of an academic bore." Nia smiled broadly as she said it. The irrelevance of the academic culture to the gritty realities of business was a standing joke between them.

"That's not what I ordered!" A grating voice carried across the small room.

Nia turned and saw a man in a dark suit berating a female barista at the counter. The man had a beautiful head of chestnut hair, and it took Nia a moment to realize he was wearing a toupee. His reddened face was taut and snarling, and if it hadn't been for the Brooks Brothers, he might have looked like a toupee-wearing street fighter.

"What is wrong with you?" barked the man. "I don't want your steam. It's nothing but a gimmick."

The barista took the beverage and smoothly dumped it somewhere below the counter, took a fresh cup, and began preparing another, her face impassive.

Nia turned back to Eleanor. "Why do you suppose some people yell at counter help?"

"Because they can," said Eleanor.

Nia nodded and played with the paper insulation sleeve on her coffee cup. She wondered if the yelling man, as obnoxious as he was, was somehow more honest than a man like Allen, who was always perfectly self-controlled but kept secrets.

When she looked back at Eleanor, she thought she discerned sadness in the older woman's eyes. "Are you OK, Eleanor?"

Eleanor sighed.

Nia waited for her to speak. She caught a snatch of conversation from the next table, "... maybe posttraumatic stress disorder..."

She wondered if the person at the next table was talking about the yelling man. She resisted the temptation to turn to look at him again. He was silent now, so he'd probably got what he wanted. No, he had probably got what he thought he ordered. He would never get what he wanted.

Finally, Eleanor took a sip of her coffee. "My term on the Novarum Board of Directors is expiring, and I've decided to make a change in my 'day job' as well."

From the overhead speakers, a jazz saxophone sounded a bleating note, like a goose being strangled.

"You're leaving the university? I thought you loved being a dean."

Eleanor smiled wistfully. "I've enjoyed most of the role. And I wasn't actively looking for a new position. Restless, perhaps, but not initiating anything other than the usual networking we all do as a matter of course. Witmer-Kelly contacted me and after a bit of persuading I agreed to be wooed by the private sector. After several interviews and a lot of reflection, I've decided to accept the COO's position with a pharmaceuticals firm. So of course I can't continue to sit on Novarum's board."

"I don't understand." But even as she said it, Nia realized she did understand, and only too well. Eleanor was abandoning her.

She looked down at the table. Time slowed, and Nia knew she needed to say something to keep the conversation going, but she could think of nothing to say. She felt like Eleanor was breaking up with her. What would she do without her mentor's protection?

"It won't affect the Turkey project," said Eleanor.

Like hell it wouldn't. The line came unbidden to Nia's mind. How could Eleanor do this after all they'd been through together? She could hear a muted trumpet from the sound system. Chuck Mangione's "Feels So Good." It had been a long time since she'd heard that song. It was wildly inappropriate, as if someone had switched on the wrong soundtrack. She almost wanted to laugh—almost.

"Nia, say something."

Nia looked up. Eleanor was watching her.

"What is there to say?"

"You could wish me luck or say you were happy for me."

"Good luck," said Nia. In her own ears, her voice sounded flat. She realized she was goading Eleanor because she was angry.

"Don't you see?" said Eleanor. "This is the best possible time for me to leave. You have the Turkey project. I've accomplished my goal of getting the company to adopt strategic planning. You've accomplished your goal of having an impact on revenue."

Nia felt Eleanor had rehearsed this argument. She felt frustrated, vulnerable, and angry. It was an unusual combination of feelings, and she didn't know quite what to do with them.

"You're worried about Allen, aren't you?"

"Wouldn't you be?" said Nia.

"No," said Eleanor simply. "Allen's on board. He sees the value in this project. He has taken ownership of it. And he knows you're the heart and soul of it. He's not going to jeopardize it."

"He's already reprimanded me for going over his head," said Nia. "I think he's angry. And I think I'm going to be on the receiving end of that anger."

"What is it you think he's going to do?" said Eleanor. "The project's already budgeted, isn't it? At least half the Board is behind it, and all the outside directors are. In his own interests, Allen is bound to make this thing succeed, and that means making you succeed."

Nia shook her head. "I don't think you know him like I do."

They were silent for a moment. Finally Eleanor spoke again. "I know him much better than you think."

Nia sensed a story coming.

Eleanor sipped her coffee, but put it aside, apparently cold now. "As you know, I have a history with Allen."

"I remember you said you worked together at Brigham & Women's in Boston. It didn't sound like a very close relationship, the way you described it."

"It wasn't. I was Chief of Residents when Allen was doing his pediatric ortho residency. That made me his boss, to whatever extent a strong-minded physician can have a boss." Eleanor smiled at her joke, then continued. "One morning an OR nurse alerted me that Allen was planning an operation on a sick child that same afternoon. It was risky for her to tell me, but I'm glad she did. I reviewed the case and concluded the procedure wasn't justified. I was technically correct and acted well within my authority when I cancelled the operation. But Allen didn't take it very well. There was no shouting or anything, but I felt the resentment in him."

"He gets very quiet when he's angry," said Nia.

Eleanor nodded. "We discussed the case in private over the next few days and he eventually conceded that his approach was probably wrong—which it clearly was. So you see, he's perfectly capable of bouncing back from something, even something he considers a personal affront. And he's not one to hold a grudge either. After all, he was the one who brought me on to the Novarum board."

Nia tried to imagine Allen and Eleanor as much younger. Eleanor was probably in her thirties then. Allen could have still been in his twenties. "Was there no other fallout?"

Eleanor shook her head. "No. Every time I've dealt with Allen since then, he's been the soul of professionalism and consideration."

Nia digested Eleanor's story. She couldn't find anything cautionary in it. Every business, even health care, is rife with conflict and tension. Eleanor's take on this made it sound like Allen managed the conflict well, even as quite a young man.

"Where's your new job?" asked Nia.

"Rotare."

"At their HQ in Raleigh?"

"Yes. We'll have to meet virtually."

"At least you'll never have to worry about ulcers," said Nia.

"That's what's interesting," said Eleanor. "They want my experience in patent restoration. Finosec's patent is expiring."

Nia was glad for this news. Novarum Pharmaceuticals had no product in the ulcer control market. She would not have liked to be competing directly with Eleanor.

"Do you have any advice for me on dealing with Allen?"

Eleanor thought about it for a moment. "Don't try to hide anything from him."

"Why do you say that?"

"He's pretty good at finding the lines of communication." She shifted herself in her chair. "I don't know how he does it, really. But about a year after we had our set-to over the child's operation, I had an occasion to see the OR nurse who brought the thing to my attention. She told me her relationship with Allen was not the same after the incident. I had promised her confidentiality when she alerted me, and I kept it. But Allen apparently found out she was the informant. While he never confronted her and he remained cordial, she said she could sense him straining, and he never gave her tasks again but always asked for help from someone else.

"I never learned how he had ferreted her out. But he had a strong motivation. He was much younger then, and—forgive me if I sound biased—he had the ego of a young physician. That's the way medical education was in the 1970s and '80s. A student spends 11 years being told he is a part of the selected few and pretty soon he starts believing it. But they generally get over it. It's part of the job of the Chief of Residents to help them, which is why I disciplined him the way I did."

Her story finished, Eleanor sat back.

"You're sure he's over all this?" said Nia.

"Of course," said Eleanor. "Didn't he ask me to sit on the board? What better proof that he's forgotten all about it? He's the CEO and this isn't the 1970s. He's had many years to grow up."

Nia gazed through the window at the activity on the street outside. The choreography of thousands of business professionals trying to get their coffee and get to the office always awed her. It was surprising how little jostling occurred in this flow of decorous humanity. Then a familiar dark-suited figure separated itself from the crowd of commuters. His posture suggested an attitude of score-settling as he bore in toward the very shop in which she was seated. It was the man with the hairpiece.

* * *

Once again, Ward and Allen were seated at the small conference table in Allen's office, meeting with a third executive. Ward felt far less comfortable this time, because they were meeting about Temel Ilac, and the third executive wasn't Nia. It was Rasheed, Novarum's CIO. Allen had mentioned something about the meeting proceeding easier without Nia, and Ward couldn't shake the feeling they were meeting behind her back.

As was generally the case a couple decades ago, IT at Novarum was once part of finance. But shortly after Allen arrived at Novarum, Ward realized it was too large for him to manage out of his back pocket any longer. When his IT people began to clash with the computer support staff over in R&D, Allen ordered him to merge the two information systems. Ward realized it was time for a specialist, so he hired Rasheed to run the new consolidated unit. He chose Rasheed because he was one of the most agreeable and courteous people Ward had ever met, and Ward knew the merging of the systems would require a consummate diplomat.

Rasheed had done an outstanding job. After he'd been in the job a few months, new desktop systems began appearing in many departments, together with staffers to install them and coach people in their use. Classes were offered on security and widely used applications. Network outages stopped. Departments began to take delivery on long overdue systems. Support calls throughout the company were answered within minutes, problems resolved within hours.

Within a year, Ward had elevated him to the position of CIO. Rasheed, although the youngest director in the company, had a remarkable grasp of the big picture, yet he had such tact and deference that other executives all seemed to think he was fulfilling their goals. He was so good at this, in fact, that he rarely saw the inside of Allen's office. As a director, he was a sort of junior member of the executive committee, and it was understood that Ward supervised his work. The infrequency of Rasheed's dealings with Allen doubtless explained the nervous smile he wore this morning.

Allen nodded at Rasheed. "Let's hear what you have."

Rasheed, who had large wet spots at the armpits of his shirt, opened his laptop. He turned it so Ward and Allen could see the screen.

Allen leaned across the table and gently closed the lid of the laptop. "I don't want to see another PowerPoint. I just want you to tell me what's going on and how you feel about it."

Unlike Nia, Rasheed seemed shaken by Allen's display of power. Ward wished he had warned him about Allen's aversion to PowerPoint.

"But I have it all here." Rasheed's voice was soft and raspy.

"I don't want a presentation," said Allen. "Just give it to me straight, and don't sugarcoat it. Whatever problems you've found, I want to know about them."

"But there are no problems," said Rasheed. "I've never seen a trading partnership work so smoothly. Even the EDI. I expected Temel Ilac would be on the U.N. standard, EDIFACT. But they were set up for X12 as well."

Spouting abbreviations and acronyms seemed to calm the young man, and although Ward was inclined to let him babble, he wanted to understand what Rasheed was saying. "You'll have to explain some of these terms," he put in.

Allen glanced at him impatiently. Did he understand this jargon already?

"Oh, sure," said Rasheed. "EDI is the way we exchange data between organizations. There are two standards. X12 is what we use most in North America. EDIFACT is what they use in the rest of the world."

"Is it a computer language?" From the corner of his eye, Ward saw Allen tapping his pen on the table surface. Ward understood he was wasting Allen's time and he resolved to ask no more questions.

But Rasheed, if he noticed Allen's impatience, seemed incapable of restraining himself as he launched into a comprehensive explanation. "Maybe more like a codebook," he said. "It's a set of terms everybody uses to represent different kinds of communications between us, like purchase orders, invoices, and stuff like that. I expected these guys to be using the European codebook, and I thought we would have to set up a translation system between the two, but they are able to use our codebook already. It's as if they were bilingual."

Allen seemed to brighten at this. "What if they get their codebooks mixed up?"

"I don't think there's much chance of that," said Rasheed. "I work with a guy there who trained at Michigan State. He worked here in the U.S. for several years. He knew X12 before he learned EDIFACT. He knows the difference."

"You don't think there's any possibility of misunderstanding?" said Allen.

"Misunderstandings are always possible," said Rasheed, "but I worry less about this guy than most. He and I read all the same magazines and Web sites. We communicate very well."

Ward couldn't hold himself back from bringing up his own pet concern. "What about security?"

He could see Allen nodding in support of the question.

"What about it?" said Rasheed.

"Do they observe our standards of security? Are you satisfied with the way they safeguard data?"

"They're at least as good as we are about that," said Rasheed, "probably better."

"There must have been glitches or problems somewhere along the way," said Allen.

"No," said Rasheed, "none."

Ward thought he detected a note of pride in the young man's voice. He was pleased for him.

"No slipped deadlines?" said Allen. "No misunderstandings? No budget overruns? No leaked trade secrets?"

"None of that stuff." Rasheed was completely calm now. "I've never had a better experience with a partnering organization. My counterpart even taught me some new things." Rasheed absently dusted the cover of his laptop with his shirt cuff. "He showed me a way to avoid the clearinghouse and exchange data over the Internet."

It seemed to Ward that Allen was digging for problems and finding none.

In fact, Allen received Rasheed's recitation in silence, as if he were disappointed.

The three of them sat silently in the hush of Allen's office.

"Wait a minute," said Allen at last. "Did you say you were exchanging data over the Internet?"

"Oh, yes," said Rasheed. "Much cheaper than the clearinghouse, and it can be reached from anywhere in the company."

"Or from anywhere in the world." Allen's voice contained a hint of alarm. "What about hackers?"

Rasheed laughed again. "We use strong encryption and secure sockets. If anything, the data is safer on the Internet than it would be going through the clearinghouse."

Ward had only the dimmest idea of what Rasheed was talking about, but he'd never known the young man to make a bad technical decision before. Nevertheless, he shared Allen's concern about the Internet.

"Are you comfortable using the Internet for this?" said Ward.

"Completely. I'd bet my job on it." Rasheed looked from Ward to Allen. His smile faded at what he saw in their faces.

"I won't let you risk your job, Rasheed," said Allen. "I don't care what Temel Ilac tells you about the security of the Internet. You're going to move the data exchange back to the clearinghouse."

Rasheed looked anxious again. "I checked with Nia on this before I went ahead." He wiped the top of his laptop with his shirt cuff again. "It's perfectly safe. If we change now, it could set the project back by thirty days or more."

"Thirty days' delay is trivial compared to the security of our data," said Allen.

"Please," said Rasheed. "I can show you articles and white papers proving this is safe."

"Do you have one that shows the average cost of a data breach?" said Allen.

"Well, no. I—"

"It's five million dollars," said Allen. "There were over three hundred documented data breaches last year, and probably a lot more that were never reported."

Ward was surprised Allen had this information at his fingertips. It was as if he'd studied up on it before the meeting.

"I'm aware of that," said Rasheed. "But there's nothing that makes this system any less safe than the clearinghouse."

"I'm glad things are going so well with the project," said Allen. "But we're going to use the clearinghouse. We've used it before. We know it's safe. I have a board of directors to answer to."

Rasheed began to speak one more time, but Allen held up his hand.

"Thanks for bringing this to my attention. Please give me regular progress reports on the change, and make particular note of any resistance you get from Temel Ilac."

"But I know my client will be upset about this."

"You can refer Nia to me."

Instructor's Resources

Learning Goals

Based on reading this chapter and knowledge of leadership and organizational behavior theory, students will be able to

- discuss the challenges and methods of "managing up," that is, ways one can influence one's superiors on critical issues
- evaluate the proper role of a mentor who occupies a higher position in the hierarchy than the mentee's supervisor
- describe the realistic and hoped-for behavior that a subordinate expects from her or his supervisor
- begin to explore the concept of bad leadership.

Discussion Questions and Possible Instructor's Responses

Q1 ***What does Rasheed's nervousness tell us about his suitability for leadership?***

He's apprehensive and may lack confidence with others, including his subordinates. He might have an external locus of control and possibly esteem issues. The CIO role requires a full range of leadership competencies beyond the threshold of technical expertise. In working with superiors, the leader must be able to effectively persuade and negotiate. Rasheed's reluctance to engage in a more spirited but respectful debate is a troubling characteristic. It may reveal a fissure in his character, that is, the desire to seek harmony rather than insist on arriving at the best possible technical solution to a critical issue.

Q2 ***Is Allen communicating fully his concerns about data transfer?***

Based on what we are learning about Allen, his line of questioning would suggest he has an underlying motive that hints at bad leadership. That is, he appears to be seeking a legitimate reason to halt the Temel Ilac project. However, his concern about information security is beyond reproach, so speculating about his motives must be done with caution.

Q3 ***How would you characterize the mentor-mentee relationship between Eleanor and Nia?***

Eleanor appears to have good intentions and the best interests of Novarum, Allen, and Nia in mind. Her willingness to be an advocate and gatekeeper for Nia is derived first from her belief that Novarum needs to become a global player. She encouraged Allen to hire Nia because she thinks Novarum is strategically vulnerable. She justifies her less-than-forthcoming conversation with Allen about the source of the Temel Ilac partnership as a business necessity. And certainly Nia was grateful for the help. Still, she has put Nia in a difficult position vis-à-vis Allen.

For her part, Nia has considerable respect for Eleanor and views the relationship as essential to her success, even survival, at Novarum. In this respect, one could argue that the relationship has become too enmeshed. The mentor may have overstepped her bounds.

Q4 ***Does Allen harbor a grudge against Eleanor?***

We do not know. Eleanor's critique occurred years ago, and Allen did recommend Eleanor for a seat on Novarum's Board. Eleanor states that she doesn't think he is petty. Still, the way Eleanor omitted details may have resurrected some bad feelings in Allen. His trust in Eleanor may have been breached, perhaps irreparably. Because they are not trying to clear the air, the possibility of restoring trust is very low, if not nil.

Q5 ***Is technical expertise and having the facts on one's side sufficient to gain acceptance of a desired course of action?***

To Rasheed's dismay, it appears not. He is more technically savvy than Allen regarding IT issues in general and IT security in particular, a point that Allen implicitly concedes. Allen is relying on position power rather than best practices and objective truth to defend his decisions.

Rasheed's frustration with Allen may reflect naïveté. In an ideal world, the technically correct answer should prevail. In the typical formal organization, however, hierarchy still concentrates power at the top. Rasheed is a technocrat, and his method of persuasion is data-based. Allen's unlikely to be swayed by facts, even though he uses facts to bolster his argument. The myth of rationality is revealed here: Allen has intense negative affect about this proposed project. Perhaps his real position cannot be altered by cautious but incisive questioning by his two executives. It certainly won't be altered by arguing the facts.

Q6 ***What else might Ward and Rasheed do to influence Allen's decision to use the Internet rather than a clearinghouse for data transfer?***

Possibly nothing. On the other hand, while the hierarchical concentration of power won't wither away any time soon, it is slowly eroding due to two general trends: (1) In the aftermath of WWII, there has been a growing consensus in the academy and corporation of the superiority of participative management over autocratic styles. It is now more acceptable to question authority, albeit respectfully. (2) With the introduction of user-friendly Web browsers in the 1990s, bureaucracies flattened as employees gained easy access to information that was previously closely held by the executive suite. In the first decade of the 21st century, the democratization of information was accelerated by self-organizing communities expressing themselves through open-source programming, wikis, blogs, social networking sites, all facilitated by wireless communication devices. To the extent that information is power, decentralization and egalitarianism have ascended. No one individual can claim to have all the answers when the wisdom of the masses can be easily harvested and compared with any individual's version of truth.

Given these two trends, Ward and Rasheed may have tried interest-based, rather than positional bargaining with Allen. At this point, neither man understands Allen's underlying motives. However, they're dubious of his espoused rationale. Perhaps they could tease out Allen's agenda through open-ended questions. If the issue is ego, they may be able to help Allen save face and bring a worthy project to the market. Allen may be angry, but he's not self-destructive. If Ward and Rasheed can appeal to Allen's ego, and perhaps instill a bit of anxiety about the need to keep up with the competition, they may be able to devise a plan that puts Allen's stamp on the project. That plan might involve a fast Internet search of best practices beyond the two options under current consideration. The three may also find another country for clinical trials in addition to Turkey. Many options exist when a group focuses on underlying interests and moves off of positions. With additions to Nia's plan, Allen could at least claim it as partially his. How he would handle that with Nia is a concern, of course. He can still proceed with the project, as ordered by the Board. Making it his project rather than exclusively Nia's is perhaps the only way Allen will sign off.

In the meantime, one must assume that the facts rarely speak for themselves. Rasheed has the facts, but Allen has the power.

Q7 ***How do you view Ward's behavior during the meeting among Allen, Rasheed, and him?***

Ward appears suspicious about Allen's line of question, but remains silent. He does nothing to support his CIO, even though he believes in Rasheed's technical expertise. Ward may have remained silent because he doesn't know enough about data security to argue for Rasheed's proposed method for data exchange. But assuming the method is standard protocol, Ward should have been reasonably comfortable with Rasheed's plan. Therefore, he could have asked Allen to be more forthcoming—in a diplomatic way—about his concerns, and tried to allay them. Ward's silence serves neither his boss nor his subordinate well.

One could interpret Ward's silence as either self-protective or strategic. In the former case, he simply wants to survive; in the latter case, he may be waiting for an opportune time to question Allen. Or Ward may have an agenda fueled more by personal ambition than an interest in Novarum, Allen, Nia, or Rasheed. So, as with Allen, the question of Ward as a bad leader should be raised.

4

Suspenders with a Belt

Rasheed was wary. When he and Ward entered the office, Dr. Hanna wasn't over at his conference table. He was seated at his desk and gesturing at the two chairs across from it. It felt like being called to the principal's office.

"What's up, boss?" Ward smiled, but his body looked a little stiff when he lowered it into the chair. "Haven't seen you in nearly two days."

Dr. Hanna didn't return the smile. Instead, he gave Ward and Rasheed each a copy of a document—output from the color laser printer that served the executive suite. About a dozen pages, it had some stylized futuristic color photos on the front and looked like one of those downloadable whitepapers so ubiquitous on the Web. It was titled "Imperatives and Precautions" and had the subtitle "Encryption Standards and Data Security for the New Millennium." Rasheed was familiar with the firm that published it. It was a firm that sold data clearinghouse services and VPN software. Web networking had been eating this firm's lunch for the past 5 years. They published a whole library of these papers intended to scare businesses out of using the Internet for EDI.

The Varieties of Leadership at Novarum Pharmaceuticals: A Novel, pages 65–77

"As you know, I've had an abiding concern about the Temel Ilac project because of data security," Dr. Hanna started.

Rasheed thought he could see what was coming and tried to head it off. "My staff is working on the conversion to the data clearinghouse right now."

"Tell them to stop."

A feeling of relief washed over Rasheed. "Have you decided we should stay with the Internet?"

Dr. Hanna stood up abruptly and paced behind his desk.

Rasheed's feeling of relief gave way to a discomfort he would not have been able to name.

"No," said Dr. Hanna. "I've decided the clearinghouse protocol isn't safe, either."

"But..."

Rasheed had begun to speak without thinking, and he caught himself, wondering what he had intended to say. Dr. Hanna considered himself a scientist. It would be impossible to contradict him without questioning his understanding, and with a man like him, that could be risky. Dr. Hanna was good at grasping management problems, but he knew squat about technology. Right now, Rasheed's chances of convincing him that Novarum could communicate securely with Temel Ilac were nil. Dr. Hanna would dismiss anything he said as the ravings of a computer geek. He didn't need to argue with the man right now. He needed to buy time.

Fortunately, he didn't have to follow up on his "but," because Ward was talking.

"How are we going to exchange data with them?" said Ward.

Dr. Hanna waved his copy of the article. "This article confirms my greatest fears. Temel Ilac's IT architecture is not safe enough for me to entrust our IP to it."

Rasheed knew better than to shake his head, but he wished people would recognize when they were out of their depth.

"This paper explains that data clearinghouses are really no safer than the Internet. They generally use the exact same protocols and standards."

It was the same thing Rasheed had tried to tell him at the last meeting. But apparently it was more believable coming from a colorful 12-page paper he'd downloaded from the Web.

"I don't claim to understand the details," said Dr. Hanna, "but the executive summary is clear. No system is absolutely secure. The best thing encryption can do is to require an intruder to use so much computing power that it wouldn't be worth the effort."

This was certainly true. The whole idea behind encryption was that a code needed to be able to withstand assaults long enough that the information being protected was useless by the time the adversary obtained it. The usual standard was 1,000 years. In fact, given the patent law, there really wasn't anything at Novarum Pharmaceuticals that needed to be protected more than 17.

"The paper," continued Dr. Hanna, "says that an algorithm called OTP can provide absolute protection. The only cost is that it doubles the size of the message, since the decryption key is as long as the message itself. Given the computing power available to us, I think that cost is trivial."

Rasheed groaned inwardly. OTP, the so-called "one-time pad," dated from the days of the KGB and flash paper. Yes, it is secure, but so is wearing a belt with your suspenders. If he had to implement this, Deniz and Serdar at Temel Ilac would wonder what prescription drugs were being dispensed to whom.

"The key is generated randomly for each message," continued Dr. Hanna. "It's actually quite ingenious."

"What do you propose we do?" said Ward.

"First, Rasheed, you and your most technically current staff should read—no, peruse—this white paper. Next, contact Temel's people and explain the situation. Immediately follow that conversation up with a detailed document that describes OTP as our new encryption standard. Be sure they understand this is a nonnegotiable condition."

"Dr. Hanna," ventured Rasheed, "OTP requires that we find a secure way to send the random keys."

"I'm sure you'll be able to come up with something," said Dr. Hanna.

"But don't you see that the need to communicate the key opens another vulnerability?"

"I don't see it's any less secure than public-key encryption."

“Exactly,” said Rasheed. “It doubles the workload without substantially increasing security. That’s why nobody uses it.”

Dr. Hanna sat down again. “I’d have thought you’d jump at the chance to be on the leading edge.”

“With all due respect, sir, this is not leading edge. To get the benefits of OTP, we must physically transport the key. We’ll be FedExing CDs to Turkey every day. Where’s the security in that?”

“You’ll just need to find a way to communicate the key electronically.” The look in Dr. Hanna’s eye said he was finished arguing about it.

Rasheed was left with a choice no man should have to make: between keeping his job and looking like a fool among his professional peers.

* * *

“I’m sorry Ms. Stevens, Mr. Deniz is not available.”

Nia looked up at the departure schedule display. Her flight to Kennedy, miracle of miracles, was available for boarding on time. She started toward the gate with her cell phone pressed to her ear.

“May I speak with Mr. Serdar?”

“Mr. Serdar is not available, either.”

“This is my third call. What seems to be the problem with their availability?” Nia added before the woman could respond, “Why hasn’t either one returned my call?”

“I’m very sorry, Ms. Stevens. I do not know the answer to your question.” Then, silence.

She had no more than a moment before she reached the security checkpoint, but Nia wanted to keep the conversation going. She had to get to the bottom of this. “Are you sure they received my calls?”

“Of course.”

Did Nia detect a note of disdain in her voice? Couldn’t be. Nia was Temel Ilac’s biggest account. It must be a translation problem. She made a mental note to look into Turkish intonations to see if that might tell her anything.

“Temel Ilac,” continued the woman, “prides itself on its conscientiousness. I assure you I gave your messages to both Messrs. Deniz and Serdar. Is there anything else I can help you with?”

“Please be sure they understand I must speak with either one immediately. You do have all my contact information, correct?”

"Yes, I have your land line, cell phone, and e-mail address," the woman answered evenly. Do you wish for me to repeat the numbers?"

"That won't be necessary."

Nia ended the call and submitted to the inspection at the security checkpoint. At least her flight was leaving on time. Thank God for little favors. Or whomever. It would be good to get to New York. Maybe she'd have time for some personal business.

* * *

When Ward arrived for the meeting with Allen, he found him working with, of all things, a PowerPoint file. Had Allen finally discovered how useful PowerPoint could be? He couldn't decide if his boss was demonstrating flexibility or imbalance.

Allen had used the program to "draw" an organization chart. It was an attractive chart, but it didn't look much like the Novarum Pharmaceuticals Ward knew. There were boxes he'd never seen before, and Strategic Planning was attached to it as kind of an adjunct.

Ward knew Allen was preoccupied lately with what he had begun to refer to as "the Temel Ilac fiasco," but this was clearly something he'd been working on for months. Perhaps it was a contingency plan he'd designed to better align strategy and execution and to respond to Board pressure to emphasize global business. He knew Allen better than to think it was some kind of punishment of Nia, whose function appeared nowhere on this chart. The new global sales and marketing division would make a strong statement of strategic intent and get the Board off Allen's back. But what about Nia?

"But what about Nia?" said Ward.

"I wanted to make sure Nia would still be able to influence foreign business," said Allen, "so I have attached her unit to GSM."

GSM? Ward realized it was the abbreviation for Global Sales and Marketing, which had a prominent box in the chart.

"Is Nia reporting to GSM?"

"Not reporting, exactly," said Allen. "She's part of Administration, and this dotted line just shows her interface with GSM. She interfaces with other departments also, but I didn't have room for all the lines. She'll have a lot to manage as a planning function for the other units, so I've preserved her executive rank, and we'll increase her salary by twenty percent."

Ward wondered how much of this was a plan and how much a hope.

"I've managed to line up Terry Armstrong as EVP of GSM." Allen looked as if he'd won a spelling bee. "He's a marketing wiz with a master's in international business from Wharton."

Ward knew Allen well enough to know he shouldn't stop him at this point.

"The exact details of Nia's new role and title," said Allen, "will get worked out after the new EVP of GSM defines what is necessary to succeed. Armstrong has deep experience. I'll rely on him to tell us what is essential in the job. Nia's job description will become the natural complement. Therefore, no role conflict between the two EVPs. Everybody wins."

"Does Nia know about the reorg?"

"Not yet. She's in New York. I think she may have trouble getting back with the storm on the east coast."

"What about tomorrow's investors meeting?"

"I'll just have to give her apologies for her. That reminds me. I want to send her an e-mail with the good news."

"Good news?" asked Ward.

"Indeed. Promotion. Twenty percent raise. Who wouldn't be cheered by that?"

Ward said nothing.

Allen continued with his explanation.

"Here's the other important part of the plan: outsourcing. As you may recall, I attended an all-CEO outsourcing conference early this year. An expression was often used at that conference: 'creative destruction.' Are you familiar with the concept?" Allen asked. Any MBA would have at least a passing understanding of Schumpeter's thesis that capitalism is essentially dialectical, acting and reacting, tearing down and building up, introducing and retiring products, services, and even industries, creating jobs while sending out termination notices.

"You can't make an omelet without breaking eggs?" offered Ward while wondering where Allen picked up all this dialectical business. If the analogy gave Allen pause, he didn't probe for more understanding. Ward concluded this was not the time for witticisms.

"I'm thinking we should capitalize on the disruptive energy of the reorganization. Here, read this draft memo and tell me what you think."

It unnerved Ward to feel Allen staring at him as he scanned the page. And in fact, he didn't read it so much as absorb certain signals that set off his personal alarms, like the boldface capitalized label across the top: "CONFIDENTIAL." He sensed that Allen was trying to enlist him in some sort of secret undertaking. Ward was always nervous around conspiracies.

He picked up other signals: "multiyear contract," "outsourcing," "Excelsior Consulting, LLC." Wasn't that the outfit that had a worldwide reputation for facilitating the gutting of American companies? Didn't he read somewhere they were the bozos that convinced his credit card firm to move its customer service operation to Obscuristan? He wondered how Becky was doing.

His misgivings were not allayed as he scanned further. The first function Novarum was going to outsource was human resources. Excelsior was going to move it to Mumbai, India. How could anyone in India understand salary, vacation, sick time, and insurance benefits formulated in Evanston, Illinois?

One thing Ward absorbed word for word: Allen expected to save $37.5 million over the life of the 10-year contract after subtracting one-time transition costs. That was a lot of scratch. At $3.75 million a year, it would provide a lot of cover in case business went south. On the other hand, doesn't it send the wrong kind of signal to your employees when you ship their records and their benefits counseling to Asia? What were the costs of that?

But Ward had other things he wanted to understand before he asked Allen about such costs.

"What's going to happen to our HR staff?" he said.

"Many of them will get the opportunity to bid on other positions in the company," said Allen. "Those who can't or won't fit themselves in with our strategic direction will get industry-competitive severance packages and assistance finding other employment."

"What kind of assistance?"

"Excelsior has a career services unit, and as part of the deal, I got them to include a 60-day package for every Novarum employee who needs it. They get personal counseling, access to a job-hunting support group, and a Web site that includes substantial resources: everything from a business library to a full complement of self-assessment instruments."

Whenever presented with a proposed change of this magnitude, Ward found it wise to give himself sufficient room to maneuver. Like all successful executives, he knew how to simultaneously express support *and* noncommitment. It's a good skill to have when your CEO asks for your reactions to a *fait accompli.* Still, he struggled to figure out something to ask that might get Allen to pause in what seemed a headlong plunge into this plan of his.

"You're talking a lot of jobs, many of which are union," said Ward. "How do you think Bud Wolinski will respond?"

"About what one would expect from a union president who learned the business in the sixties and keeps an autographed picture of Jimmy Hoffa hanging on his office wall.

"In fact, about half of the positions are nonunion, so an ULP won't stick. But I'm sure Bud's people will start building barricades when he gets word of this plan. His people will be given the standard nonexempt package."

Ward looked down at the memo again. "Why Mumbai?"

Allen smiled. "This is the beautiful part. Excelsior has a subcontractor there with an English-speaking workforce."

"I don't doubt it," said Ward. "But Mumbai? People in Mumbai will be handling our 401(k) contributions and tracking our vacation time? Doesn't that strike you as strange?"

"Ward, this is the twenty-first century. It's nothing more than a customer-service function. Excelsior has had great success with that in everything from credit card operations to software support."

Ward shook his head.

"What's wrong?" said Allen.

"What do we know about India?"

Allen sighed. "All we need to know is that it has a highly skilled workforce, dedicated to growth through capitalism."

Allen was talking, but he apparently couldn't hear himself.

"Do you have some kind of racial bias against India?" said Allen.

Alarm bells sounded in Ward's head. "Not at all. Not at all." He shook his head vigorously. "All I meant was what if they have a war there? The border between India and Pakistan is a tinderbox. And internally, India has enormous challenges: vast illiteracy, crushing poverty, primitive infrastructure outside of the cities, an out-of-control population and, despite the illegality, a defacto caste system. Then there's the Muslim problem. One-hundred-fifty million people with almost no economic mobility and little chance of integrating into the larger Indian society. Isn't this a rather insecure environment for our personnel files?"

"Nonsense. It's a very stable society and becoming more prosperous all the time. Mumbai, Bangalore, Chennani, and Hyderabad are IT hot spots. Foreign direct investment is pouring in. The Indian Institutes of Technology were ranked third best in the world for technology universities according to the *London Times*. Indians are bursting with entrepreneurial energy. America's stereotypes are badly outdated."

Ward digested this, then tried to follow it to the next step. "Why are you starting with HR? Don't you think we'll need them to bring the employees around to all this?"

Allen looked at him seriously.

"I've long felt that the department is not fully trustworthy," he said.

"What do you mean, trustworthy?"

Allen's voice was soft but it had a discernible edge.

"I think salary information has been leaked to those without a need to know. In my experience, little is more corrosive to an organization than disclosing personal financial information. It destroys morale and teamwork because people make inaccurate comparisons about their inherent worth and contributions. That's why we make it a terminable offense. I suspect it was someone in HR who did the leaking, but whether it was or not, the staff there is responsible for the security of that information, which makes them responsible for the leak."

"Do you have any proof?"

"I don't need proof," said Allen. "This is a reorganization, not a disciplinary action."

Ward could feel his arguments being chipped away from under him. He nodded. "The memo hints that not everyone will be given the opportunity to bid on other jobs within Novarum. Have you decided who's not making the cut?"

"Not entirely, but certainly some HR supervisors will have to be terminated immediately—with a severance package, of course. Excelsior's been around the track. They're good at handling the human fallout from an outsourcing project."

"Why immediately?" Ward asked.

"Certain people have access to too much vital and confidential information. We can't take a chance on these key people tampering with data sets in some nonobvious ways. Excelsior tells me that lower-level staff does not know enough to sabotage computer files without being immediately caught. Hence, they don't. Not so with smart supervisors who really know our personnel and IT systems cold. They could create all sorts of nasty logic bombs that might take months to detect and never leave a fingerprint."

Reorganization, outsourcing, unions, Nia—Ward felt stressed and not unmoved by Allen's reasoning and prescription. Novarum did face strategic challenges. Loss of the Novarum patent would devastate P&L for years. Globalization appeared inevitable to many and rich with opportunity. Analysts and investors had been expressing concern for increased overhead. Excelsior had a talent for extracting employee productivity. American labor unions whined, no matter what management did or didn't do. And, for whatever complex set of reasons, Nia appeared incapable of establishing an international alliance. Maybe Novarum did need to transform itself with just such a bold plan. But with all these thoughts racing through his mind, Ward could think of nothing to say that was fully rational. So he settled on something that he thought Allen would consider an endorsement, but for which he held something of a promise to himself he was being ironic. "Seems like you've thought of everything," he said.

But Allen didn't smile. He closed the PowerPoint file, took the memo back, and put it in an unmarked folder. "I hope so."

Instructor's Resources

Learning Goals

Based on reading this chapter and knowledge of leadership and organizational behavior theory, students will be able to

- discuss the impacts of emotion on decision-making, disguised sanctions and bad faith, and bad leadership
- evaluate some of issues involved in outsourcing jobs to a foreign country.

Discussion Questions and Possible Instructor's Responses

Q1 ***Is Allen's decision to move, yet again, data transfer from the clearinghouse to OTP justified?***

Uncertain. Some will view it as a very thinly veiled aggressive act by Allen designed to prod Temel Ilac into killing the project, while holding him innocent. Others may view Allen's act in a more favorable light. He may sincerely believe he is acting in the best interests of Novarum by elevating the standard for data security. After all, he possesses a technical report to support his case. In a dangerous world, caution is an admirable trait. Those who see Allen's motives as mixed, or base, will interpret the technical report as a convenient cover, giving Hanna plausible deniability.

Bad leadership can be conceived of in different ways. Barbara Kellerman (2006) conceives of bad leaders along a continuum of ineffective to evil. In the business world, I prefer a 2X2 matrix of effective (yes or no) and ethical (yes or no). Of course, a binary classification scheme is reductionistic. Still, it gives us a way to think about bad leadership in two dimensions. A bad business leader is easier to classify, i.e., one who is both ineffective and unethical, e.g., Al Dunlap (Sunbeam), Leona Helmsley (Helmsley Hotels), Bernie Ebbers (WorldCom), Ken Lay and Jeff Skilling (Enron), Denis Kowalski (Tyco). Classifying Allen may present students with a more difficult choice, at least at this point in the story. For example, one could argue that Allen should reside in the unethical but effective quadrant because while his motives aren't pure, his decision to keep Novarum's data secure is a prudent business decision that could save the company from serious problems.

Q2 ***Although it's unclear at this point whether Temel Ilac is sticking with the agreement, would it be rash if it were to withdraw?***

It is axiomatic that one shouldn't make important decisions when angry. Apparently the firm has made an abrupt, unilateral decision to withdraw from the partnership. If Temel Ilac's executives interpret Novarum's most recent demand as irrational, they might want to try reasoning with their potential partner before giving up. If they view Novarum's behavior as ethnocentric, they are undoubtedly angry *and* insulted. Not a hopeful way to view a prospective partner. Temel Ilac may be wise to terminate the relationship. But they may want to attempt one more meeting to agree on all manner of operational issues starting with data transfer. If so, they should insist on having all of Novarum's stakeholders in the room, physically or virtually.

Q3 ***Is Allen's reorganization justified?***

It looks suspicious. With the Temel Ilac proposal, Nia is already doing what Allen envisions the GSM EVP is being hired to accomplish. Why create two groups doing essential the same work? On the other hand, he may have lost some, but not his entire faith in Nia. And yes, he probably is angry. But perhaps he does believe that she and Terry Armstrong will work well together, and their complementary roles, even if more redundant than complementary, will produce synergy. It is also possible that their roles might produce healthy competition.

Maybe Allen wants to humble Nia a bit, but not humiliate her into resigning, or overtly terminate her contract.

Q4 *Is outsourcing justified?*

Even if Allen's motives aren't pure, Novarum will save millions by outsourcing. Big Pharma is under pressure to cut costs (See "Pharmaceutical Industry: Background" for details.) But the fallout from the unions and exempt staff may be costly. Still, one could argue that in addition to saving money and improving service, Novarum will gain local knowledge in India, which can only help them when they explore ways to penetrate the vast Indian market for their drugs. At some point, India could well be a service provider and consumer for Novarum.

5

Dancing with the Team

Rasheed noticed that in the aftermath of their meeting with Dr. Hanna, Ward did not suggest a postmortem. That was fine with him.

"Rasheed, get on my calendar when you've pulled together an action plan." Ward pushed the button to summon the express elevator.

"Okay."

Rasheed didn't wait around for the elevator with his boss. He preferred the stairs. When he pushed open the door into the stairway, he was relieved to find himself alone. He was baffled as to what the action plan might be. He embraced the engineering profession's values of logic and efficiency. Evidently the health care profession operated from a different set of values. Otherwise, why would his superiors—Ward included, apparently—devise such a half-baked plan? Better tell my management team now and get this over with, he thought. No need to ruin a three-day weekend by ruminating. But what could he say to this crew?

Rasheed's eight direct reports represented a full range of IT functions. Like any group that works together for some time, they had established

The Varieties of Leadership at Novarum Pharmaceuticals: A Novel, pages 79–100

favored routines, friendships, and factions. And it didn't take him long to detect the informal hierarchy within the group. In the main, though, they got along well enough, tolerated individual quirks and respected each other's ability to manage the technical demands of a large assembly of computer scientists, IT engineers, systems analysts, and programmers. Novarum also had an in-house, around-the-clock help desk, advertised as ITRx, and known by Novarum's cognoscenti as T-Rex. At a staff meeting very early in his tenure, Rasheed mentioned that he liked that snappy sounding label, until Natalia asked him why he found the comparison between Novarum's help desk and an extinct species attractive. Rasheed had to concede the point, even if he didn't appreciate her sarcasm. Outsourcing was blowing like a cold wind through the IT business, and even something as innocent as a nickname could seem fraught with significance.

Still, surveys showed customer satisfaction with IT services running high. This was a cause for cheer within the team and confidence for their job security within Novarum. Ward gave his version of a compliment to the team at the annual holiday party by announcing, "As computer geeks go, you folks are very personable." Rumor had it that upon hearing Ward's remark, Dr. Hanna spontaneously whispered to Nia Stevens, the new strategic planner, "Now there's a phrase maker for you."

Ward's observation notwithstanding, two of the eight team members—Natalia and Richard—demonstrated excellent technical *and* people skills. They had also both lobbied Ward very hard for Rasheed's job before he was hired. But after two exhausting interviews—and a frosty encounter with the IT team — Rasheed found himself on the short list.

Rasheed had realized he had an inside track as a result of being the only outside candidate. Ward told him after he hired him that he'd been reluctant to promote from within the existing team, realizing that managing former peers is tricky. An outsider supervisor is something of a blank slate. No scores to settle. No enemies yet. And Rasheed had enough organizational savvy to understand that someone from outside the organization is especially dependent on, and grateful to, the selecting official. Gratitude is the foundation for building loyalty, and Ward obviously prized loyalty in his subordinates.

Rasheed hoped he carried three additional advantages over the internal candidates: age, gender, and ethnicity. Through a friend of a friend in the HR department, he learned that he was younger than his competitors, and his recent master's degree in computer science gave him cutting-edge knowledge of emerging IT research. But he had also reached another conclusion by scanning Novarum's internal personnel directory. The IT department employed very few employees of Middle-Eastern descent. While controversial and never openly discussed, ethnicity was still considered when making selecting decisions among equally qualified candidates. It could be the differentiator, he thought, even if did make him slightly uncomfortable to think it would, or should, be a criterion for hiring.

Negative stereotyping of Middle-Easterners in America was a fact of life, made all the more so after September 11. Well before passenger airplanes were turned into weapons, however, Rasheed learned that the sensible path to career mobility in corporate America was to emphasize one's similarity, without renouncing one's core identity.

"Being bicultural" was the term-of-art favored by the Career Services office. At the university's career fair, Rasheed attended a concurrent session titled "The Brand Called You." Here they told him the story of Ralph Lifshitz, a poor Jewish boy from the Bronx. The entrepreneur built his fashion empire by appealing to those who aspired to be a part of the self-assured, materially successful world of an idealized Ivy League. Rasheed wanted to join the club. So he adopted the RL style of dress and tried hard to behave in a manner befitting the generic corporate leader: steady, optimistic, tactful, open-minded, appropriately assertive, conscientious, and secular. But, unlike Lifshitz—later Ralph Lauren—Rasheed never considered changing his name or denying his heritage. "Rasheed Asadel Madhdabi" might be difficult for the generic corporate types to remember or pronounce, but they would just have to deal with it.

Rasheed might think he had 45 years of labor law behind him, but he was not so innocent as to think age, gender, appearance, race, ethnicity—and God only knows what else—didn't play some indefinable part in who gets the phone call from HR and who gets the thin envelope.

He had been introduced to an intriguing concept at the career fair regarding the state of majority-minority relations in America in the early part of the 21st century. Alert "minority" applicants could strike an implicit bargain with employers without actually saying, "I will willingly conform to corporate and mainstream social norms and give you the benefit of the doubt that you are not prejudiced. In turn, you will confirm my assumption by granting me membership into your organization and fair treatment thereafter."

To Rasheed this seemed an eminently reasonable way of living in an exceedingly diverse world at a most contentious time. It made his life more satisfying and successful, and he never felt as though he was compromising anything of significance by presenting himself in a certain way at work.

Those in authority appeared appreciative of his bearing and not a little relieved that he didn't display the hypersensitivity of an aggrieved class.

Until the train wreck of a meeting with Dr. Hanna, Rasheed liked his job—at least one part of his job anyhow. He clearly enjoyed the practical nature of IT. Business computing problems had boundaries and by rigorous thought and methods, could be solved. Not so the other part of his job: people. The open-ended nature of human wants made it impossible to satisfy and keep satisfied, one's subordinates. And that included supervisors. Especially supervisors.

In his quiet moments, Rasheed wondered if he had the right stuff to manage others. While he endeavored to behave in ways befitting a manager, he sometimes felt exhausted by the role. Did he worry too much? Was he too accommodating? Did he struggle too much when saying no to subordinates, even when he was in the right? Was he politically agile enough to build coalitions and avoid unwinnable showdowns? He wondered why his preferred style of persuasion via technical logic rarely won the argument. Others seemed to use power without much friction. Why not he? These questions were topic one of his discussions with confidants.

Holding at bay these deeper concerns about his suitability for leadership, he had an immediate hurdle to clear: how to explain to his direct reports Dr. Hanna's decision. The problem was made acute by his relationship with Natalia and Richard. Neither person fully accepted him as their legitimate boss. Even though they had competed against each other for the director's position, they remained friends, united against him.

Despite being the target, Rasheed was forced to admire the various ways they communicated disapproval. The repertoire of verbal and nonverbal criticism included the ever-so-slight sharpness of tone, slow responses to requests for information, withholding information until directly asked, making witty, irreverent but largely irrelevant comments during meetings that others found funny but disrupted the workflow, putting Rasheed in the difficult place of either laughing and thus reinforcing their acting out, or not laughing and being viewed as priggish. Rolling of eyes and deep sighing to suggest his proposals revealed incredible naïveté was another favorite, along with crossing arms, barely covered yawns, doodling, minimizing eye contact and never encouraging him even though he often publicly praised team members for their exemplary work.

And the most impressive part of the act was the way in which both of them calibrated their behavior, adjusting it when he appeared ready to reel them in. He withheld reprimanding the duo because he wasn't certain that his perceptions wouldn't appear baseless to HR, making him look thin-skinned and weak. Plus, he doubted that the other six members would corroborate his claim. After all, Natalia and Richard had worked at Novarum for years. How could he convincingly argue that they were poisoning the group climate when the team seemed to work well together? Maybe the other six team members resented him for reasons he would be hard put to identify or understand. All eight enjoyed good relations with their key customers. Moreover, they displayed professionalism, cooperativeness, and a *can-do spirit, doggone it,* when interacting with Ward. To add another layer of complexity, Ward, Natalia, and their respective spouses had a regular golf foursome going. Rasheed stumbled upon this tidbit when he inquired at the regular Monday staff meeting as to how everyone's weekend was. And how had Rasheed spent the weekend? The question was never asked.

Into this climate Rasheed had to explain to his staff that they would have to make another 180-degree turn in the Temel Ilac project. Marching orders this time required the team to design a method of information exchange that was outdated at best and dangerous at worst.

* * *

"You're kidding," Natalia said immediately upon hearing Rasheed's description of the CEO's decision. The team was feisty under the best of circumstances, and calling a late Friday afternoon meeting before a 3-day weekend was no way to bring out their better angels. They trickled into the conference room, requiring Rasheed to wait a full 15 minutes before he could start talking.

"Does Allen have any idea how much we've put into this project already?" Richard quickly added.

"That's irrelevant, Richard," Natalia interrupted him. "Sunk cost is just that. What's really at issue is the logic of Rasheed's proposed solution. It doesn't make sense. We will appear in *Computer Time's* "RetroAge" column.

"It could leave us wide open to security leaks. Has Risk Management signed off on this?" asked another manager.

Rasheed hadn't thought to ask that question of Dr. Hanna, so he instead responded to Natalia's characterization of the decision.

"It's not a proposal, folks. It's an order," said Rasheed.

"Why didn't you protest more," demanded Richard. "You must know this is far from best practices for data transfer."

"I did protest. I explained my concerns."

"And?"

"And what?" Rasheed let some irritation seep into his voice. "OTP is what."

"Not enough," grumbled Natalia. "Where is Ward on this?"

"On board, of course. He was at the meeting," said Rasheed. "He expects me to inform him of our new plan."

"When?"

"Soon. Very soon."

"And those plans are what, exactly?" asked another team member with an edge in his voice.

"I need your help on this. I would like you all to think about the challenge Dr. Hanna has presented us over the weekend and be prepared to discuss it at our Monday meeting. You can exchange e-mail with each other, and I will ask all of you to read the threads," said Rasheed.

"Tuesday, Rasheed," Richard reminded him. Monday's a holiday, remember."

"Oh, yes. I forgot. Thanks for correcting me, Richard."

"Anytime."

* * *

Driving at his normal speed, Rasheed typically covered the 283 miles between Chicago and the Detroit suburbs in a brisk 4 hours. Today the drive took considerably longer because he wanted time to think. He left his apartment later than planned for the weekend getaway because at the last moment he decided to send Ward an e-mail restating his serious reservations about OTP. Ward usually checked messages over the weekend, and he expected to hear back before Monday's—ahh, Tuesday's—staff meeting. Rasheed hoped he could persuade Ward to change his position, or what appeared to be his position. Ward was a hard guy to read, especially when in Dr. Hanna's presence.

* * *

As an undergraduate, Rasheed had still believed he was "one of the guys," and he often had little patience with his father, who advised him interminably how to deal with anti-Arab prejudice.

"It's not like that," he said to him one evening over dinner. "They don't treat me any different than anybody else in the fraternity."

His father grunted. "Are there any Jewish boys in this fraternity?"

"What's that got to do with it?"

"If you are unwilling to answer the question, it obviously has a great deal to do with it."

His father could be so smug sometimes.

"I don't know," said Rasheed. "There could be, I guess. We don't talk much about religion."

"Being Jewish is more than a religion," said his father.

"Can't you get over this?" said Rasheed. "We don't live over there. The fighting over there is not about us."

"I can't get over it," said his father, "because they can't."

"That's a big generalization," said Rasheed.

"The Jews claim they have been persecuted for thousands of years," said his father. "And they are right. It's only natural they have a bond among themselves. It is a bond that no one else in the world can understand—except Arabs."

"I don't want to get into that," said Rasheed. "I'm just trying to tell you why I believe I am not the victim of anti-Arab prejudice."

"And that's what I'm trying to explain to you," said his father. "Who do you think has more influence in American society, Jews or Arabs?"

"It's not relevant," said Rasheed.

"It's the only thing that *is* relevant," said his father. "I am telling you this as your father who loves you. The best thing you can do is make contact with other Arabs, particularly those in positions of influence. They will do more for you than anyone else at that university."

"Thanks for the advice, Dad," said Rasheed. "May I be excused now? I have to get over to the fraternity house."

As time went by, Rasheed realized that there was nothing special in his differences with his father. Every young man of every culture and country had to endure a period of adjustment when he grew to maturity and met his father on more equal terms than he had as a child. But by the time Rasheed had graduated from college, he had finished the adjustment, stopped arguing with his father, and even saw the wisdom in some of his observations.

* * *

"Nasseri here."

"Doctor Nasseri, hello! This is Rasheed Madhdabi. How are you, sir?"

"Rasheed. It's wonderful to hear your voice. I'm well. How are you and your family?"

"We're all doing well. Thank you for asking. In fact I'm home this weekend."

"And how is corporate life in Chicago? Are you putting your talents to work for that pharmaceutical company? Abbott Labs, isn't it?"

"No, sir. Novarum Pharmaceuticals. Actually, that is what I wanted to speak to you about, Dr. Nasseri."

"Aha."

"Yes. I was wondering if I may drive over to East Lansing and talk to you in person."

"Unfortunately, not this weekend. You were lucky to reach me today. I'm leaving soon for the airport. Tomorrow I'm making a presentation at WORLDCOMP's International Conference on Security and Management."

"Yes, I see."

"Rasheed, I have a few moments right now. Please tell me what is on your mind."

Rasheed told his former advisor all, starting with his enthusiasm about the Temel Ilac project, Nia's vision, Dr. Hanna's inconsistency, the CFO's vagueness, and the challenge of establishing his leadership within a team of difficult managers.

Dr. Nasseri listened carefully. That was one of the reasons he was immensely popular on campus and why grad students trampled each other to secure his membership on their thesis committee.

"What else is on your mind, Rasheed?"

"Nothing, really."

"Are you sure?"

"Yes. That's the whole story."

"All right, then. Permit me to tell you what I think."

"Yes, please."

"First, Dr. Hanna's right to be worried about doing business with terrorists. There are radical elements in that tough neighborhood that might well make things very messy."

Rasheed was stunned. He assumed, perhaps unconsciously, that the CEO had baser motives for the abrupt change in the Turkey project that had nothing to do with terrorism. He started to say something, thought better of interrupting the professor, and said nothing.

"The Middle East is in the midst of an enormous transformation, as is the entire world. We are not too far removed from the industrial age, and we won't know the outcome of this sea change for at least fifty years. What's certain is the world will look very different by 2050 than it does right now. But I don't subscribe to the premise that there are no more grand narratives."

Rasheed was confused but knew Dr. Nasseri well enough to know he could land this idea safely.

"What I mean is I think the world—developed and developing—is moving in a general direction of capitalism, cross-border trade, and greater personal freedom. Whether that includes representative democracy and some sort of a merger of nations, as in the EU, is another question. Still, the trend over the past hundred years suggests something like a capitalistic, democratic global society is growing. Albeit with setbacks and rearguard actions. True, there are no historical inevitabilities, but I think there is something in the body politic that seeks more egalitarian relations within and across borders, an incipient movement toward enlightened leadership and a lessening of subjugating people with traditions, tyrants, or religion. But, as I say, how the story plays out is unclear, and there are likely to be several chapters written. In the meantime, the CEO of any multinational starting business in that part of the world needs to be cautious."

Rasheed realized after a moment that Nasseri had completed the major part of his explanation and was giving him an opportunity to respond. He wasn't quite sure what part to grab on to. "So Novarum shouldn't engage in a joint venture with Temel Ilac?"

"I didn't say that. I know nothing about Novarum's strategic environment or its resources. In general, I'm in favor of cross-border alliances and think, on balance, globalization is a force for good." He added, "assuming governments, NGOs, and international labor unions don't abdicate their watchdog roles. Without checks and balances, free markets tend toward predatory practices, or at least a concentration of wealth for the favored few."

"Favored few?"

"Yes, the three hundred or so multinationals, centered in a few dozen countries, that came to the capitalistic party early."

"What about companies in the developing nations—China, India, Singapore, Brazil? They're making their presence known, aren't they?" Rasheed asked.

"Indeed. And with luck and good leadership more of the wealth created by these companies will stay at home. The world desperately needs a more equal distribution of everything of value—money, water, clean air, peace."

"Are you optimistic that this will evolution will happen, Dr. Nasseri?"

"Yes, but I think it is something of a race between the relatively comfortable few and miserable many. We counsel the developing world to be patient and let the market work its magic, guided by the UN's Millennium Goals and well-intended but also often inept help from the IMF, WB, IDB, et cetera. I'm not sure how much more patience exists in the poorer nations. But this brings us back to your CEO. From what I gather, he realistically sees the dangers of investing in the developing world. I can't know if he understands or agrees with the legitimate causes of those dangers. The West has a lot to answer for. It hardly matters. He's not running a welfare agency. From what you tell me, I assess your CEO as a businessman, concerned first for his shareholders. The social impact of your drugs and the seeding of capitalism in other places is secondary importance to him."

"What about his OTP approach to deal with security?"

"Absurd, of course."

"Doesn't that suggest he has a hidden agenda?"

"Not necessarily. CEOs are used to getting their way. Maybe he's oppositional by nature. Why can't you give him the benefit of the doubt, Rasheed? Assume his motives are financial and strategic, not xenophobic."

"Do I have a choice?"

"Of course you do."

"What? If I agree to implement the OTP, I will lose face with my team and professional colleagues. If I defy the CEO, I will get fired."

"Possibly so."

"Is that much of choice?"

"We all make compromises in life, Rasheed. The question, as I see it, comes down to this: are you being told to obey a legal order?"

"Sure. OTP is backward. Embarrassingly so. But legal."

"So, it's not illegal?"

"Correct."

"Is implementing OTP unethical?"

"How do you define unethical?"

"Would most people in the business world consider this directive from your CEO to be immoral, unfair, unjust?"

"No, I don't think so. Most people wouldn't care about what method we use. But IT people will think Novarum's IT department is bush league."

"Is it worth risking your job by not complying with a legal order from the CFO and CEO?"

"Even if I agree to the OTP, I'm worried that Temel Ilac will think that Novarum is an unreliable, maybe prejudiced partner. They may pull out of the deal."

"Can you control what others think, Rasheed?"

"Not really. Not much."

"Well, then . . ." Nasseri's voice trailed off. He was obviously content to let Rasheed finish the conclusion for himself.

"Dr. Nasseri, I have another problem at Novarum. My management team."

"Ah, yes."

"To be honest, I think they're bothering me more than Dr. Hanna."

"And that is because . . ." asked Dr. Nasseri.

"They constantly challenge my authority. I've tried to be supportive, collaborative, inspirational, charming, logical, ingratiating. They grudgingly follow my orders. And two of them, the ones I bested for the director's job, verge on hostility. I'm losing my patience."

"With them or with the job?"

"Both, I suppose."

"And if these two 'troublemakers' weren't on the team? Would your feelings change about the team and/or the job?"

"Probably. Yes."

"And OTP?"

"If I had a team that supported me, we could figure out a way to implement OTP and save face. Maybe buy time until Dr. Hanna and Ward come to their senses."

"So then the principal cause of your dissatisfaction is the people management?"

"I suppose so. Yes."

"Then why haven't you confronted these two in particular and the team in general?"

"Because then they really won't comply with my directives."

"As the director of IT, are you getting enough of what you need for the unit to succeed?"

"Yes. Our customer satisfaction scores are high."

"And what about you? Are you getting enough from them to succeed?"

"Yes, I suppose."

"Then why are you entertaining handing in your resignation?

The line was silent while Rasheed contemplated that contradiction.

"Rasheed, what do you think motivates people at work?"

"Money, status, growth, novelty, competition," Rasheed shrugged.

"The usual suspects," smiled Dr. Nasseri. "Anything else?"

"Punishment?"

"Without doubt. Much good work is accomplished in organizations because people are afraid of losing status, income, or coming in second. We're attracted to the light, but we also fear the dark. Maybe more so."

"So what are you saying, Dr. Nasseri?"

"What are you afraid of, Rasheed? Really?"

Rasheed swallowed before answering, "That they won't like me if I give them direct orders and punish them for not complying."

"Do they like you now?"

"Probably not."

"And are you getting what you want from the team now?"

"No."

"Then, what choice does that leave you?"

* * *

Jenna arrived at her sister's house, as planned, in time for breakfast Saturday morning. Lydia looked ready for anything in her kayaking outfit of jeans and plaid flannel shirt, and Jenna admired the healthful, outdoorsy glow her older sister wore. As a result of Jenna's job, it had been months since the sisters had done anything together, and Jenna looked forward to a lazy day on a calm river, even though she felt it was time stolen from work. Frank had never given her the "all clear" for this weekend, so technically she was still on call. Feeling defiant, however, she had decided to keep the date with her sister.

The two women unloaded the box containing the new roof rack from the back of Jenna's van.

"Let's open it out here so we can get the instructions," said Lydia. "Then you can read them over while I serve breakfast."

It sounded like a good plan, so Jenna used her Swiss Army knife to cut the tape on the end of the box and open the flaps. Fortunately, the instruction booklet was right on top, but as she took it out, she got a glimpse of a tightly packed arrangement of metal tubes and struts. And the phrase "assembly required" echoed in her mind.

She must have looked concerned, for her sister patted her shoulder.

"Don't worry about it." Lydia pushed the carton behind the van where it wouldn't be visible from the street. "We'll figure it out." Then she started up the steps into the house.

Lydia, like Jenna, possessed no particular skill at mechanical work, but she had much more confidence around tools and components, and Jenna had come to realize that was mainly what you needed. After all, the manufacturer of this thing would not have been able to stay in business if it only sold its products to engineers.

Jenna followed her sister up the steps with the instruction booklet.

In Lydia's sunny kitchen, Jenna sat at the table and opened the booklet while Lydia spooned up oatmeal and retrieved a pan of hot muffins from the stove. The first page of the instructions included a diagram of all the rack's parts. There was something that looked like a shock absorber and some other things that were clearly the sides of a sort of cradle that Jenna supposed would hold the kayak's hull. There were straps and buckles and hooks. But there were lots and lots of bolts: knobbed bolts, U-shaped bolts, and a lot of more conventional-looking bolts that appeared to require a hex driver. Fortunately, there was a hex driver listed among the parts as well.

"I had no idea this would be so complicated," said Jenna.

Lydia walked over with a dish of oatmeal. She set it at Jenna's place and glanced at the instruction booklet. "That's just the parts list."

"We might be here all morning," said Jenna.

"That's just for reference," said Lydia. "See what the language is like in the directions."

The directions were in three languages, but one of them was English, and the outlined steps seemed clear. But there were so many of them, it was too tedious to read the text without the relevant parts in her hands.

"I don't know, Lydia," she said.

Lydia sat at the table with another bowl of oatmeal. "Are we stuck, then? Do I have to find a man to help us out?"

"Don't taunt me," said Jenna.

Lydia smiled. "I'm just trying to encourage some of that resourcefulness you're famous for."

"But all those parts so tightly packed in that box . . ."

Lydia interrupted her. "Haven't you always told me you should think outside of the box?"

Jenna laughed. "It's a metaphor. It doesn't apply in this situation."

Lydia sipped her coffee. "Oh, no?"

And then Jenna realized there was indeed a way to think outside the box in this situation. She didn't have to be limited to the instruction booklet the company had supplied. She took her Blackberry from her backpack.

"Oh, not that thing again," said Lydia. "Are you going to call 'Kayaks R Us'?"

Jenna ignored her sister and launched the Blackberry's browser. In moments she had found what she needed: a movie on how to assemble the carrier. With the movie running, she proudly pushed the Blackberry across the table to Lydia.

Lydia laughed as she picked the thing up. "I'll be damned. This thing is more useful than I've ever given it credit for."

The Blackberry overlaid the voice of the narrator with a soft chime.

"What's that?" said Lydia.

"I've got an e-mail," said Jenna.

"Well don't look at it until we're back from our outing," said Lydia.

* * *

Ward's memo, written at 2:30 Sunday morning, was a study in abstraction and ambiguity. Rasheed couldn't tell if he did or did not support OTP. But he was clear in that he expected Rasheed to use his "considered technical judgment" to execute the order. Ward's message also conveyed a hint of irritation, and he didn't want Rasheed to bother him with more questions or concerns about the issue. Ward wanted to know that Rasheed was on the case and he would deliver results. Rasheed forwarded the message to his team without comment.

Before returning to Chicago, Rasheed checked his e-mail. He found perfunctory responses from a few team members. If they had communicated with each other over the weekend, it wasn't being shared with him. The angle of the setting winter sun made the return drive difficult.

Even so, the drive was a pleasant interlude before the meeting Tuesday morning.

"What I want to do is hear from everyone, in turn. What should we do to implement OTP?" Rasheed asked the group at the 8:00 a.m. meeting.

Silence.

"Let's start with you, Natalia. What do you think?"

"What I said on Friday."

"Tell us again," Rasheed said evenly.

"It's woefully out of date. I'm not sure Temel Ilac will agree. They shouldn't really. By 'solving' one problem we are confronted with another problem. Besides it is incredibly inefficient."

"Duly noted. Next."

Richard of course went next and pretty much echoed Natalia's viewpoint. As Joan started to speak, Richard interrupted her. "Not now, Richard," said Rasheed. "We've already heard from you. I want each person to state their position without comments from others. Joan, please continue."

Rasheed noted that the movement in the room slowed. At least one member stopped doodling. After Joan spoke—mostly agreeing with the first two—comments from the others appeared a bit more equivocal, as though people were hedging their bets because they sensed some sort of confrontation brewing in the way Rasheed opened the meeting. After hearing from every team member, Rasheed did not, as normal, open the floor to discussion. On his drive back from Detroit he had resolved to not turn the meeting into a free-for-all with nothing decided and be left without a plan and without a clear, public declaration of who was onboard.

"Folks, perhaps you didn't understand my instruction. I did not ask you if you thought we should implement OTP. That is not an option. The question before each of us is simple: how can we create a method to comply with our superiors' directive."

"Is Ward in agreement?" asked Richard.

"You'd know Ward's position if you had read his e-mail in response to mine. I forwarded both messages to all of you Sunday morning. As you should recall, I asked you to exchange e-mails offering your thoughts about this important issue. I waited until early this morning before forwarding your thoughts to Ward," Rasheed stated.

No one said anything, but the implication of Rasheed's comments was not lost on them. It would be apparent to Ward the extent to which the team was grappling with this issue. After a few furtive glances around the table, members either looked at Natalia and Richard or Rasheed.

"So, here we are. Now. And here's what we need to create by COB today: a comprehensive project plan for implementing OTP that gives the work breakdown structure with time and cost estimates for each milestone and shows dependencies by each of your functional units. It is now 8:30 a.m., and I want each of you to convene a meeting with your staff to outline your initial understanding of what must happen in your department to get this project running. We will meet back here at 10:30 sharp to merge your plans and complete the roll-ups of time, costs, and dependencies. I told Ward that we will be ready to brief him at 8:00 a.m. on Wednesday with a second meeting with Dr. Hanna scheduled for later that day. That means we won't have much time at our meeting with Ward to refine our thinking before meeting with Dr. Hanna. Thus, between now and tomorrow morning we must have a solid, high-level plan. I want everyone to clear their calendar and be back here at 10:30 with your unit's initial thoughts. Be prepared to stay late tonight. Any questions?"

Stunned silence, until Natalia spoke. "Half of my managers took a long weekend. I don't have a full staff. I can give you my portion on Thursday."

"That won't do, Natalia. Gather whatever intelligence you can from your staff and be back here in two hours."

She glared at him, but he continued speaking.

"Also, I want to stress something else. You will not 'hand in your portion' of the plan with the belief that someone else, notably me, will harmonize the plan. We are Novarum's IT management team and we will develop this plan together. Every unit's contribution will be vetted by all of us to be sure it supports the project's desired outcome. Upon completing the plan and getting top management's approval, we will, as a team, create a final plan, and each of you will then create detailed functional plans. Those plans will then be reviewed in a series of meetings where you and your team will present your functional plans to our management team. I informed Ward that we will have the entire detailed plan pulled together NLT than Friday night. And one more thing: successfully implementing OTP is a group goal. I have assigned it to the entire team and have recorded it as one of your key results for this year's appraisal cycle. No one can succeed on this project unless we all succeed. Everyone will receive the same rating. Now, are there any other questions before we break?"

Undoubtedly many had questions. None were asked. And in the Novarum rumor mill, the first meeting of the IT team after a long weekend came to be known as "Rasheed of shock and awe."

Instructor's Resources

Learning Goals

Based on reading this chapter and knowledge of leadership and organizational behavior theory, students will be able to

- describe the personality traits of an effective leader
- discuss and evaluate some of the forces—social, technological, economic, political—driving global capitalism
- discuss the perception and reality of Arab discrimination in the U.S. in a post-September 11 world
- describe the concept of organizational citizenship behavior within a work team.

Discussion Questions and Possible Instructor's Responses

Q1 Was Ward remiss in not offering to debrief with Rasheed after their surprising meeting with Allen?

Definitely. And Rasheed was remiss by not asking Ward to debrief, even if Ward's nonverbal communication suggested otherwise. Rasheed needs to gain Ward's perspective on Allen's motives and his (Ward's) commitment to Allen's directive. Rasheed could also benefit from hearing Ward's assessment of how likely this most recent change in data transfer is final. Ward should also ask Rasheed what he needs from him, and others, to implement Allen's directive.

Q2 *Using the Big Five model of personality, how might one define Rasheed's personality traits compared with the ideal leader?*

To bring order to the many facets of human personality philosophers, physicians and psychologists created several typologies over the millennium. The Five-Factor model, or Big Five [neuroticism, extraversion, openness to experience, agreeableness, conscientiousness], emerged over the past two decades as the best conceptual tool for categorizing and measuring personality.

Big Five Model of Personality Related to Leadership and Applied to Rasheed

Factor	Traits	Ideal Leader (generic)	Rasheed's personality
Neuroticism (aka emotional stability, adjustment, negative emotionality)	Worry	Little	Plenty; excessively seeks approval
	Anger	Little	Little to some (perhaps internalized)
	Interpretation of events	Optimistic	Realistic with some tendency to pessimism
	Rebound time from setbacks	Rapid	Slow; ruminates; may hold grudges
	Confidence	High	Moderate to high insecurity
Extraversion	Warmth	Moderate to high	Moderate to high; a nice man; loyal
	Sociability	High	Reserved at work
	Energy mode	Active	Active; can be a bit hyper when stressed
	Taking charge	Fully	Somewhat
	Trust of others	Somewhat	Somewhat
	Tactfulness	Straightforward but not blunt	Courteous; formal; diplomatic
Openness to Experience	Imagination	High	Moderate
	Systems thinking	Sees big picture	Sees big picture; readily sees multiple causes and effects
	Comfort with change	High	High; creates change; energized by innovation
Agreeableness	Altruism	Some	Much; giving; kind; generous; empathic
	Compliant	Little	Moderate to high; accommodating; puts others' needs above self
	Reticence	Little—enjoys spotlight and figurehead role	Somewhat shy
Conscientiousness	Competence	High	High
	Order	High	High
	Dutifulness	High	High
	Achievement striving	High	High
	Self-discipline	High	High
	Deliberation	Moderate	Very high

Q3 ***Does Dr. Nasseri give Rasheed sound advice?***

Maybe not. Through his Socratic questioning, Dr. Nasseri leads Rasheed to the conclusion that he has no other option but to give his team direct orders. However, as any outsider, Dr. Nasseri can't fully understand the context in which Rasheed works. For example, he has no idea how connected Richard and Natalia are to Ward. As a tenured professor and state employee, Dr. Nasseri may not be able to appreciate how tenuous is the employment contract in the private sector. Further, Nasseri doesn't probe Rasheed as to the extent of his positional power. True, Rasheed is the CIO, but he reports to an CFO who appears to be cautious, reluctant, and averse to challenging the CEO. In this environment, giving orders may gain apparent compliance followed by substantial blowback.

Q4 ***What is your assessment of Dr. Nasseri's worldview on the likely emergence of liberal democracy and capitalism?***

No one knows if his guardedly optimistic observations are probable or even plausible. In fact, the professor's hopeful outlook is reminiscent of social commentary from the first decade of the 20th century. Many believed that international trade, made more practical by the telegraph and steam-powered cargo ships, would bring peace and prosperity to an interdependent world. Much was written about the reinforcing nature of technological and human progress that began in the European renaissance, gained currency in the Enlightenment and was expanded further in the Industrial Revolution. Nationalistic aggression was thought to have been trumped by markets and self-interest. WWI brought an end to that pleasant fantasy. The enduring attraction of fatherland and empire was demonstrated a mere generation later, followed by 50 years of "cold war." When the USSR astonishingly imploded without a bloodbath, political analysts wondered if this finally signaled the "end of history," i.e., the diminishment of nation states in favor of individualism and enlightened egoism. Looking back from September 11, 2001, some commentators declared the 1990s as a decade-long holiday from history.

Tyrants and terrorists may prevail. Globalization is not inevitable, does not necessarily bring benefit to all the participants and may even be a significant cause of terrorism in traditional societies who understandably fear annihilation of their cultures.

Still, international institutions formed in the aftermath of WWII have endured. For example, the concept of a common currency in Europe was thought mad when first proposed. Democracy, full or limited, now covers some two thirds of the world's population. Autocratic rulers are less able to insulate themselves from a wireless world. The trend line appears to be upward, but not linear. In an uncertain world, one hopes for the best and prepares for the worst. Businesses are smart to engage in global markets and wise to keep a balanced portfolio.

Q5 *Is Ward's ambiguous e-mail to Rasheed effective and fair?*

No. He's hanging Rasheed out. But Rasheed should insist on more clarity, or at least send Ward an e-mail stating his plan and asking for a reaction. In the absence of a reaction, he will assume that Ward agrees with his approach. That way, Ward is at least tacitly approving the plan.

Q6 *Is Rasheed's conduct in the second meeting with his IT team effective? How might you behave differently, if at all?*

While understandable, it is probably not wise. Rasheed drew a public line in the sand. He could have requested Ward to attend the meeting. He also could have individually confronted Richard and Natalia and required each one to become more supportive or leave the department. In doing so, he would probably want the advice of the Human Resources department and possibly present each individual with a draft or official performance improvement plan. Rasheed may send a copy of the plan to Ward, or at a minimum, discuss his intentions with Ward. He needs to get Ward on his side, and HR could be the honest broker to help Rasheed get his boss to become more supportive. As it stands, Rasheed is out there on his own, confronting two well-connected subordinates. Even though Rasheed is their formal superior, Richard and Natalia have influence owing to their technical competence, length of tenure, political cunning, and connection to Ward. Rasheed may chafe at their immaturity and bad faith, but he needs a more thoughtful, less reactionary approach to dealing with the subordinates. Being nice didn't work. Giving orders won't necessarily work either. Other options exist. Rasheed needs to find them. Giving orders should be the last resort of a leader.

6

Chant of the Chorus

On arriving at Kennedy, Nia called Pierre Casson at Witmer-Kelly, the search firm. She knew Pierre from a previous discussion. Witmer-Kelly specialized in health care executives, and about the time she was deciding to leave Galenic 2 years earlier, Pierre had contacted her about an opening at a Novarum competitor. She declined his overtures but kept his business card and promised to stay in touch. The idea of working at Novarum without Eleanor's protection made her want to consider her options.

Pierre professed delight at knowing she was in town.

After concluding her meeting with an institutional investor on Wall Street, Nia cabbed uptown to Pierre's office on Park and 37th. Pierre offered her tea with grace and solicitude. She allowed herself to enjoy his obvious regard for her.

Successful headhunters read people well. Nia knew that Pierre understood there was far more to it than the "informal chat because I'm in town" explanation she had given him. She made some vague references to having differences in strategic intent with Novarum, but she could tell Pierre was

The Varieties of Leadership at Novarum Pharmaceuticals: A Novel, pages 101–115

trying to calculate just how deep the story ran. She dressed it in business jargon, but she assumed he'd had enough of these conversations to know there were personal issues.

Be that as it may, Nia knew exactly what she had to offer: noteworthy academic credentials, business acumen, the right age, appearance, willingness to relocate, and the proper balance of femininity and sharp elbows to survive at the C level. She was also an attractive candidate, and she knew he would be happy to have her in his office regardless of her story.

They did a dance familiar to anyone in business: two people make a tacit agreement to discuss one thing while communicating about another. The verbal part of the conversation is eminently forgettable. The important communication is at the level of feelings.

"Your timing is impeccable, Dr. Stevens. I know this is only a social call, but I am currently working on two assignments that might nicely fit your career aspirations and competencies."

Nia smiled at the reference to "Dr. Stevens." As a PhD, she was entitled to it, but she always felt that without third-party payment, being a doctor didn't count for much. She had once seen a New Yorker cartoon where the maître d' inquires of the person calling in to make a reservation at a swank restaurant, "A table for two at 8:00 p.m. for Dr. Bowman? Certainly. Now, may I ask, is this a medical doctor or merely a PhD?" She had shared that cartoon with Allen and thought he had laughed a little too heartily at it. But then, given his credentials, he would.

"Please tell, Monsieur Casson."

He consulted his notes, "One is essentially a lateral from your current position at Novarum: EVP for planning in an East Coast big pharma firm."

"J&J?" Nia quickly asked with a smile, knowing Pierre would not disclose a client's identity this early in the game.

Declining to take the bait, he paused, smiled briefly, and continued.

"The other position is operational and speaks more to your persistent desire for moving outside your comfort zone: Chief Administrative Officer & Director of Compliance with a mid-sized, but rapidly growing, nonprofit health care system located in the northwest U.S. It has 3,800 employees and annual revenues of $500 million."

Nia liked the idea of a rapidly growing firm, so she extracted as much detail about the latter position as Pierre was willing to give up.

"What's the timeframe for hiring?" she said at last.

Casson sighed. "As always, ASAP. But urgency is a negotiable word, even in New York."

"This could be very interesting. May I get back to you within a week, Pierre?"

"Certainly, Nia."

"Thanks. Oh, and something else. Might I ask you not to share my name with anyone at this point? Today's meeting is *entre nous,* Monsieur Casson."

"Docteur Stevens," Pierre said with a grin, "among your many other admirable qualities is the skill of the high-wire artiste."

"Thank you."

"You can rely on my discretion," said Pierre.

* * *

When Gabe arrived at Susan's apartment in Brooklyn Heights for dinner, he was disappointed to find another guest. He'd been looking forward to dining alone with Susan. The guest seemed personable, and even interesting. Because she was here in Susan's apartment on such short notice, he knew she must be a close friend. He realized, therefore, that any sign of reserve on his part would be impolite. So he made a determined effort to take an interest in the unexpected guest.

He shook her hand. "Your parents spent time in East Africa."

"Tanzania," said Nia. "They were missionaries. How did you know?"

"Your name," said Gabe. "It means will or purpose in Kiswahili."

She smiled then, in the way you might smile at an unexpectedly accurate palm reader. "They were only there a few years," she said, "but they always seemed to think of it as the high point of their lives."

"*Penye niya, pana njiya,*" said Gabe.

"Yes!" she said. "They put me to bed with that every night."

"What does it mean?" said Susan.

"Where there's a will, there's a way," said Nia.

Then the light of recognition appeared in Susan's eyes. "That explains a great deal about you. You've spent a lifetime living up to your name."

"I've never quite decided," said Nia, "whether it was a blessing or a curse."

Gabe decided he liked the woman. The evening might be entertaining after all. How often did he get a chance to impress Susan with his Swahili?

Over a lengthy dinner of Moroccan lamb tajine, couscous, stuffed grape leaves, and Spanish Rioja wine, Gabe listened to Nia talk about her work and her ambitions. She was an executive with a large drug company, and her job was to develop and implement the company's strategy. Gabe was fascinated by this glimpse of a life he knew almost nothing about.

She wanted her company to compete internationally, she said, and for a company that needed to create a presence abroad, the obstacles were innumerable. Much of the world had learned to distrust and even despise Americans over the past 8 years, and those feelings extended to American companies and trade goods. She had hit upon a plan to make and market birth control in Muslim countries, which were currently undergoing a population explosion.

"Sounds like good business," said Gabe. "Human population growth throughout the Muslim world is very high. Some demographers say that's one of the reasons for fundamentalist jihad—a continuing renewal of the supply of young, unemployed men with little hope for social mobility."

"Your competition?" asked Susan.

"Very little," said Nia, "if the method is inexpensive and easy-to-use. The market for family planning in the developing world is enormous, and Islam is the religion most common to many of these countries. Islam claims over a billion adherents."

"I read somewhere that the fertility rate for Muslim women is four point five children—even higher in some countries," said Susan. "I think the birthrate in the U.S. is about two, and Christian Europe is experiencing negative growth. Even Italy."

"It was this kind of data that steered me toward this plan," said Nia. "Given those numbers, we're convinced there is a large market, and carefully conducted surveys find Muslim women do want a reliable method of family planning." She sipped from her wineglass. "The question then becomes how best to establish the market. My answer is Temel Ilac, an Istanbul pharmaceutical firm of considerable repute throughout Turkey and much of the Middle East."

"But isn't Turkey secular?" asked Susan.

Gabe happened to know a little about this. "Officially yes," he put in, "but in practice it is overwhelmingly Muslim. I co-authored a paper about Turkey's efforts to become a member of the EU. Turkey has been banging on the European door for decades. It's a fascinating country—full of contradictions, most notably in the relationship between the military and government. The generals are deeply suspicious of the Islamists, and any social movement suggesting a regression to pre-Ataturk times invites their attention. The army even threatened to bring down the legitimately elected government because some wives of prominent politicians began wearing head scarves in public buildings. In an odd way, the army is a force for and against modernity and democracy." He realized he was getting into lecture mode, so he stopped.

"That's right," said Nia. "Turkey promotes itself as the cultural amalgam of East and West. My plan is to use this native firm, which can lay claim to a Muslim heritage, to test and market the drug. It helps that the firm is ethnically Arab. When the product is rolled out, it will be advertised with sensitivity and associated with a Middle Eastern firm. In that way, Novarum avoids blunders so common in international marketing. Even within countries, a firm can miss the target market. A recent example occurred in Turkey, where a mid-sized pharmaceutical company marketed its product by distributing thousands of informational pamphlets in doctor's offices and clinics in the Kurdish region. The only problem was the pamphlets were written in Turkish. None of the hoped-for customers understood a word. We want to blunt the criticism by the anti-American chorus by avoiding these kinds of mistakes. Moreover, establishing a positive presence in the Muslim world gives us a tremendous opportunity to sell other Novarum products, under Middle Eastern brands, naturally."

The conversation stopped then. Gabe wasn't comfortable with the direction Nia was headed.

"Did I say something wrong?" asked Nia.

"We were both at work in Manhattan on September 11," said Gabe.

Nia looked as if she'd heard this before. "Nobody from Temel Ilac was on that plane," she said dismissively.

"Come on, Nia," said Susan. "You know Gabe's not accusing you of financing terrorism, but you've got a joint venture with an Islamic Middle Eastern firm. I'm sure you've heard comments like this before."

"Oh, yes," said Nia. "You sound like my boss. He's made my life very difficult over this project."

"Maybe he has legitimate concerns," put in Gabe.

"Look," said Nia. "I'm as concerned about terrorism as any non-naïve person. But I'm not dealing with terrorists. Furthermore, I'm actually doing something about the problem. What's the best way to modernize the Middle East? Increased business dealings with the West. Right now the Islamic fundamentalists' greatest support comes from the poor. The success of this project can stimulate a virtuous circle, bringing revenue to Temel Ilac and empowering women. Controlling population in the Middle East will even lessen environmental degradation. This venture is a model for more joint ventures in Muslim nations."

The three were silent again. Gabe looked over at Susan, and she was smiling—a "you convinced me" expression. He wasn't sold.

"Are you familiar with Huntington's clash of civilizations thesis?" he said.

"Probably not, but I can guess."

"Your guess might be pretty close, but I was at Huntington's lecture at Columbia right after September 11, and I suspect the thesis is better informed than you think. Do you mind if I explain it?"

Nia took another sip from her wineglass and waved her hand in the air. "Go ahead."

"We may interpret modern history as a story of progress—industrialization, growth of the middle class, fall of communism, increasing education, democratic trends, globalized markets... all these things point toward humanity's upward march. Nevertheless, civility in a given nation is not guaranteed. Rather, Islamic fundamentalism and ethnocentric behavior is at a dangerously high level throughout the entire Muslim world.

"Consider Bosnia, Myanmar, Rwanda, Afghanistan, Iran, Algeria, and Iraq—all areas of religious or ethnic conflict. Democracy and globalization have not tempered the passions, prejudices, and intolerance of religious fanatics and xenophobes.

"In fact, the combination of democratic trends, female autonomy, and globalization poses a grave threat to traditional societies. The disorienting effects of Western-style capitalism has caused or accelerated Islamic fundamentalism. Thus, any attempt to promote capitalism in a traditional Islamic society may drive moderate Muslims into the fundamentalist camp. Your venture could actually be making the problem worse."

Nia shook her head. "I have to believe that raising people's standard of living and binding them into modern society is salutary."

"You have to believe it?" said Gabe. "Sounds like faith-based business."

"Touché."

"If it's going to flourish," said Gabe, "capitalism needs social stability, internationally recognized contract law, minimal corruption, and peaceful resolution of business disputes. It can't transcend corrupt leaders. And Sharia's prohibition of charging interest is even incompatible with the financial services industry. What Huntington says is true: vibrant capitalism will not take hold in an Islamic state, at least not in a fundamentalist one."

"Tell it to the generals in Moscow," said Nia.

"What does that mean?"

"The international experts predicted communism would endure. Some of them even thought it would triumph over the West."

"A different religious history and different government," said Gabe. "Huntington said he thinks it is wrong to assume all Muslim societies can develop democratic and mature capitalistic institutions. Throughout the twentieth century many people assumed international business would prevent wars. It certainly hasn't played out that way. Trade grows every year, and it seems to aggravate conflict rather than reduce it."

"All of this may be true," said Nia. "But what's the alternative? Isolationism? Trade sanctions? Another Holy Crusade?"

"No, no, and no. Please don't conclude that because I'm sympathetic to Huntington's basic argument that I believe the wealthy nations are powerless to shape the future. Ethical international business, as you've described, is a sound response to the social ills generated by authoritarianism. What I am saying is that Western-style capitalism won't take over anytime soon, and the law of unintended consequences is going to create a lot of setbacks along the way. Expect a backlash—perhaps violent and sustained—if only from a tiny percentage of the population that resent birth control in particular and modernity in general. Many intelligent people share Huntington's view, including, apparently your boss. Does that make him a reactionary?"

"Does it sound like that's how I'm portraying him?" Nia asked.

Gabe didn't answer. He suspected the question was rhetorical, and he decided it was time to effect his orderly retreat.

"A CEO's job is to make sense out a bewildering environment," said Nia, "to interpret economic, social, and political forces, and make reasonably smart decisions to protect and grow the firm in light of them."

"And you don't think your boss is making the right decisions?" said Susan.

"He has blocked me at every turn. I managed to get the Board of Directors behind me, and he's had to get on board. But I think he's dragging his feet. He may even be planning a major move against me."

Gabe shook his head. "It sounds just as political as an academic department."

"What can I say?" said Nia. "An organization is an organization. There are power issues in every human relationship, and politics is the inevitable response to power."

"It sounds like your political struggle isn't going well," put in Susan.

"In fact, I need a reality check." Nia put down her wineglass and looked from Susan to Gabe. "I have a mentor on the Board of Directors. In a sense, she has been my protector as well. She just told me she's leaving. Given all I've told you about this project and my boss, do you think it's time for me to make a graceful exit?"

"It's unlike you to quit something you've committed to," said Susan.

"I'm thinking more of a strategic advance rather than quitting. I met with a headhunter today and he's bullish—in the near term, I might add—on placing me in a progressive firm. Why should I continue to be marginalized by a culture that doesn't appreciate my worth or ideas?"

"You must be disappointed in this job," said Susan.

"Disappointed?" Nia shook her head. "How about betrayed?"

Sympathy welled up in Gabe. "That bad?" he said.

"My trust in the company and—let's be honest here—my boss, Allen, has been breached. He assured me I was brought onboard to be a—no, *the*—key actor for strategic planning at Novarum. He hasn't been fully open with me on his agenda. He engages in half-truths rather than giving me a full explanation for his decisions. He says yes, and then no. And, as I've gotten to know him better, I'm not sure he has the capacity to think strategically. Tactically? Yes. He drives the COO nuts with his capacity to drill down on the causes of operational bottlenecks. Technically? Hell, yes. I've observed Allen lecture at a few professional conferences. He's masterful. But strategy is different. It's a delicate combination of prudence and daring. One of my subordinates has a poster in her office that reads, 'The past isn't a good predictor of future events in a world that has Alzheimer's.'"

She took a breath and continued.

"Plus, Allen often invites the CFO to our strategy meetings. Ward's a good numbers guy, and not a bad sort as a peer, but how many accountants do you know who can see beyond the next quarter's revenue and expenses? There was a just-noticeable air of condescension in their body language when I proposed this strategy."

"Sexism?" asked Susan.

"Who knows? I've heard of much worse treatment by managers of male and female direct reports. I think Allen resents my relationship with a member of the board. Then there's the pay issue, but I'm not going to get into that."

She seemed to run out of steam at that point.

"Hmm," said Susan.

"Forgive me for venting," said Nia. "I get even more agitated about this when I try to describe it. I think the shareholders of Novarum Pharmaceuticals should be too. I think Allen may be getting ready to sabotage a project of immense importance to Novarum and its customers.

"Leadership is about seeing potential business, tolerating ambiguity, and taking action. Of course the project carries risks, but the upside makes it worthwhile from a financial and social standpoint. Novarum purports to be a responsible corporate citizen. I've done careful research, vetted and nurtured relationships, detailed a plan, and conducted the financial due diligence. We can make a substantial ROI and do good in a part of the world that has been dispossessed for centuries."

Her remark summed up the philosophy she'd been describing all evening, and Gabe admitted to himself that, regardless of anything he'd said tonight, he subscribed to it too. He was sure all Western people of good will did.

There was nothing left to say. Gabe sensed the evening was about to end.

"I've found this conversation both stimulating and illuminating," he said to Nia.

To his surprise, Nia reached over the table and squeezed his hand. "So have I." She looked at Susan. "He's pretty smart. And he plays well with others. I like him."

Susan laughed. "He's OK, I guess."

"Thank you for dinner," said Nia. "Can I help you with the dishes?"

"Don't worry about it." Susan jerked her thumb at Gabe. "The professor here will help."

Nia seemed relieved. "I can't miss my flight. We have an investor meeting tomorrow."

They stood, and Susan left to retrieve Nia's coat.

"I wish you luck, Nia," said Gabe, "with both your project and your job. The world needs more people who think about how their work affects the rest of us." He meant it.

"Thank you." Nia gave him a kiss on the cheek. "Right now, I need some luck that the planes are still flying tonight."

* * *

Susan felt good about the evening. She was sympathetic to Nia's problems, but she had confidence in her friend's ability to handle them. What made the evening seem a great success, however, was the way she and Gabe got along. She saw Nia kiss him when she left, and she took that as a sign of her approval.

She took the wet dish Gabe handed her and began drying it. She had assigned him to the washing, since she was the one who knew where to put the dishes away. And she liked the way he wore an apron without any self-consciousness or hint of embarrassment. He was a picture of domesticity as well as confidence.

"Nia's an energetic, forceful person," he said. "It was a real pleasure to meet her."

Susan opened the cabinet and put the now-dry dish on the top of the stack. "She's a dear friend. And you see how intelligent. She was one of the very few students in our graduate program to hold her own with the professors. She told the truth to power years before Anita Hill stared down the Senate Judiciary Committee. Still graduated on time too."

"But apparently not this time. It sounds like she's hit the wall at Novarum." He handed her another dish.

Susan took the dish and wiped it. "It appears she's gotten herself into a test of wills with the CEO. That's a pity, because the project's merits should be the deciding factor, not who is the boss. What a drama."

"The gripping tale of a CEO running a publicly traded, major pharmaceutical company who puts ego and personalities ahead of investors," said Gabe.

"A Greek drama."

"Not Greek," said Gabe, "Shakespearean. Greek writers attributed human suffering to the gods. For Shakespeare it was men—ambitious, proud, naïve—who caused their own troubles."

"I hope not," said Susan. "Shakespearean tragedies leave nothing but bodies."

"You're right," said Gabe. "I don't think her situation is life-threatening. All the same, I hope she endures."

"I've never known her not to land on her feet."

"She's right that the stockholders are the ones who will suffer," said Gabe. "They'll never know what hit them, until their dividends are reduced."

Susan put the dish in the cabinet. "I wonder if the CEO has a parachute stowed somewhere."

"Golden?"

"I've never really understood that metaphor," said Susan. "A human being couldn't survive a jump with a parachute made of gold."

"They never do," said Gabe. "A CEO in disgrace, even one with a great severance package, is rarely heard from again."

"No," sighed Susan, "but they live like kings. Royalty always prevails, doesn't it, Herr Professor?"

Gabe laughed. "Kings don't always win. Think of Charles I, Louis XVI, Tsar Nicholas. And even when they do win, they don't sleep soundly."

"I wonder how Nia's boss sleeps."

Gabe stopped washing and turned to her. "How would you sleep if you were her boss?"

"I don't think I'd have any trouble."

"Have you ever managed an employee as intelligent and willful as Nia before?"

Then Susan remembered Alec. "Once." She almost shivered at the memory of the stress. "I fired him."

Gabe looked surprised. "No. Really?"

She nodded. "I've always felt bad about it."

"What happened?"

"My boss hated him. Alec spoke out at meetings, and he never pulled any punches, even when responding to the ideas and remarks of superiors. It was like he was always spoiling for a fight. I tried to get him to tone it down. My boss pressured me constantly to rein him in. Eventually, my boss sat me down and told me that my department couldn't have two leaders and I had to do something about him."

"Tough situation," said Gabe.

"After I fired him, life went back to normal. But I've always wondered if it wasn't my responsibility to protect him from the higher-ups. After all, I didn't really have any issues with him myself."

"You've always been tolerant of disagreement." Gabe handed her another dish. "That's the last one. You know, I think you'd probably sleep pretty well in his place."

Susan put the dish in the cabinet and hung the dish towel on its rod. "Speaking of sleeping . . ." Her voice trailed off.

Gabe took off the apron hastily. "I'm sorry. I've overstayed my welcome."

Instructor's Resources

Learning Goals

Based on reading this chapter and knowledge of leadership and organizational behavior theory, students will be able to

- discuss some of the thought processes that enter into making career decisions
- take into consideration the "clash of civilizations" thesis to evaluate the wisdom of a major U.S. pharmaceutical firm doing business in nations with a Muslim majority population.

Discussion Questions and Possible Instructor's Responses

Q1 ***If you were Nia, would you contact an executive search firm while in New York City?***

Probably yes. From a career management standpoint, it is advisable to appear satisfied with and committed to one's current employer, yet open to overtures from others and alert to opportunities. Meeting with Pierre is a sound gesture because she is already in town and they have a positive prior relationship. Plus, the chilly and ominous reception Nia most recently experienced with Temel Ilac would give one pause.

However, Nia should guard against appearing too eager in her meeting with Pierre. More deeply, she should be wary of sabotaging herself at Novarum. At this point, she occupies a prestigious, executive role in a major firm. Even if the Temel Ilac deal blows up, she may have enough social capital within Novarum to launch other projects. And she's learned a lot about Allen's worldview that can only help her in pitching other strategic proposals. According to Eleanor, Allen doesn't hold a grudge and, prior to the Temel Ilac speed bump, her relationship with Allen had been positive. So she may be unconsciously, prematurely concluding that her career at Novarum is finished. It may not be, unless it occurs by her own hand.

Q2 *Nia conveys to her friends that she has been marginalized, even betrayed, by Allen, with Ward acting as an implicit accomplice. Do you agree with her assessment of the situation?*

Perhaps Nia is right. In her view, a view held by Eleanor and other board members, Nia's proposal is beyond reproach, yet her boss won't support it, ostensibly because he lacks vision and may harbor ethnocentric and sexist attitudes. Thus, she is being rendered impotent. Her feelings of betrayal derive from the understanding of the role for which she assumed she was hired: EVP of Strategic Planning.

On the other hand, she has only been with Novarum 2 years, her proposal is bold, and her track record at Novarum is insubstantial. Allen's concerns about data security are not all wrong, as even Dr. Nasseri suggests. Plus, sometimes the best way to handle a career setback is through patience, not anger, reactivity, and exit. Allen's motives might not be pure, but she might be holding him to a higher standard than is realistic for a CEO.

Q3 *What does the Huntington thesis have to do with Novarum?*

Plenty. In addition to Dr. Nasseri's observations, consider the following:

> It should have come as no surprise, then, that Muslim reaction to the attacks of September 11, 2001 tended toward the euphoric—in striking confirmation, it would seem, of Huntington's bold thesis. Nor is the phenomenon of "Muslim rage" directed against America alone. In Spain, the Netherlands, Great Britain, France and Germany—countries with widely varying foreign policies toward, and colonial histories in, the Muslim world—terrorist plots, terrorist attacks, spectacular murders, and mass rioting have made vivid the gulf that separates embittered and often radicalized Muslim minorities from the democratic societies around them. (Bret Stephens "How to Manage Savagery" *Commentary*, Sept. 2008. v.126, i.2.)

After 9/11, Samuel Huntington's 1996 book, *The Clash of Civilizations and Remaking of History*, attracted many supporters beyond conservatives. Even some liberals had to wonder if a fundamental schism existed between the Muslim theocracies and Western democracies. The argument laid out by Gabe holds that liberal democracy is alien to authoritarian nations, especially those in the Muslim world, even if they embrace capitalism. (Think China, Saudi Arabia, Iran. All seek profit, yet none permits democracy.) Because democracy is a more enduring form of government than one-party rule—secular or theocratic—a Western corporation takes a greater risk in establishing a business relationship with a Muslim partner. Further, Huntington believed that the West was in decline vis-à-vis China and the Muslim world, and the fault line of civilizations—Christianity vs. Islam—would be conflict-laden. Huntington said, "The centuries-old military interaction between the West and Islam is unlikely to decline. It could become even more virulent." (S. Bret, *op.cit.*)

The counterargument is that capitalism can coexist with Islam, especially in the relatively enlightened, developing nations, e.g., Turkey, Indonesia, UAE, where the separation of religion and business is accepted in practice, if not formal policy or political rhetoric. Furthermore, intra-Muslim conflict dates back centuries. And Europe has a long, dreary history of war within its Christian borders. Thus, conflict is not limited to a single cause, i.e., differing religions or forms of government.

Capital seeks stable markets. In the long arc of history, war has occurred everywhere under many religions and rulers. We in the West believe that democracy, separation of church and state, free-market capitalism and decision making based on the scientific method produces the most benefits and causes the least harm to consumers, investors and society. In this basic assumption, Allen and Nia are undoubtedly in agreement.

The sticking point for the joint venture derives from Allen and Nia's relationship, but it is complicated by the particular nature of the proposal with a Muslim country. Would Allen have nixed the proposal for a joint venture if the partner were, say, Italy?

7

Who Said Anything About Reprisal?

At JFK, Nia saw the weather had delayed her flight to O'Hare. She should have gone to American's Flagship Lounge, where it was quiet and she might be able to work, but she was exhausted from the trip and from reliving all her problems at dinner with Susan and Gabe. If she found her departure gate, she could probably get some time to herself while she waited to see if the plane would be flying at all. She found the gate, which looked empty and even a little forlorn. Laughter echoed from a bar nearby.

Standing here among the empty chairs, she no longer wanted to be alone. She went in and had a seat at the bar.

The bartender put a napkin in front of her.

"What do we have in the way of bottled water?" she said.

He reached under the bar and pulled out a bottle. "Mavi." He lifted an eyebrow at her, then looked down at the bottle and began to read the label. "Exceptionally pure and singularly clear, drawn from the ancient springs of Istanbul."

Nia laughed. "There are no ancient springs in Istanbul."

The Varieties of Leadership at Novarum Pharmaceuticals: A Novel, pages 117–128

"How do you know?" He smiled, and Nia could see he was bantering with her.

"I've spent time in Istanbul. Nobody ever pointed out any springs."

"Maybe they keep them secret from tourists."

"I didn't go as a tourist."

"That's your problem." He nodded at the laptop she was carrying. "Too much work. Not enough tourism."

Nia laughed. Maybe he was right.

"Do you want the water?"

"Can I get it with lime?"

A glass appeared in front of her. He squeezed a lime wedge into it, then opened the bottle of water, filled the glass halfway, and set the bottle beside it. "Enjoy."

Nia sipped at it and picked up the bottle to look at it. There was a color picture of Hagia Sophia on the label. The water tasted good—substantial, somehow. She refused to take this as a sign.

With the bartender gone away to attend to someone else, she became aware of the other voices around her. Eavesdropping is nearly unavoidable at a crowded airport bar, and Nia didn't even try to tune out the other conversations. Besides the usual chatter of nervous, tired, and restless patrons, she began to pick up fragments of a story that captured her attention. A trio—two men and one woman about her age—were seated at a table about eight feet behind her. They were loud, the way people will be at the end of a successful trip. They congratulated each other at length, and Nia discerned after a time that they had just returned from Jakarta, where they had signed a contract. From their toasts—to preschoolers of Indonesia and their deficient diets—she eventually gathered their firm had partnered with an Indonesian firm in the same way Novarum Pharmaceuticals had partnered with a Turkish firm. Their partner would be supplying vitamins and dietary supplements to Indonesian preschoolers under license. The pilot project would reach several hundred thousand children over 5 years. Nia stared at the wood grain on the surface of the bar to screen out other distractions.

"Here's to Dr. Prawiro," said one of the men.

"Dr. Prawiro," his companions exclaimed.

"May he prosper and may his Health Ministry bathe in the gratitude of Indonesia's families for their well-nourished children."

"May he prosper—" said the other man.

"And the rest of it," said the woman.

"And may he see the wisdom," sang out the second man, "in approving a well-crafted proposal for supplying prescription drugs to the government of Indonesia, its workers, and their dependents."

"Shhh," said the other two.

The three of them dissolved into laughter.

When the laughter finally stopped, one of them proposed another toast. "Here's to Suparman."

"Suparman."

"Suparman. The best CEO this side of Krakatoa."

Nia recognized the name Suparman and realized they were from Rotare. Suparman was Javanese. She wondered if that gave this company an edge in dealing with the Indonesian government. Indonesia has a population of over 200 million. That would probably put the number of government employees and their families in the millions. No wonder these folks were celebrating. It sounded like they had the inside track to the pharmaceutical sale of the decade. She felt like the second place finisher at a race.

"How's the Mavi?"

She looked up. The bartender was standing in front of her.

"Exceptionally pure and singularly clear."

He laughed. "Good one." He laid a chit on the bar beside her and left.

She looked at her watch and saw that she had used up most of American's projected delay. The chit said the water was five dollars. She left a ten on the bar, collected her laptop and her coat, and started toward her gate.

The three executives at the table were still talking animatedly. They were probably running on adrenalin. Who wouldn't be?

Had Nia ever considered nutritional supplements? It was a market every bit as compelling as birth control. And why hadn't she thought of Indonesia?

She headed toward her departure gate and saw a few people milling around in the seating area. Bad sign. And when she got to the counter, her misgivings were confirmed. Her flight was cancelled.

There was no one at the counter, but Nia was used to dealing with travel hassles. She took her phone out of her bag and got on the mobile Web. It took less than 2 minutes for her to learn, much to her dismay, that *all* flights to O'Hare were cancelled. Nor was there anything to Fort Wayne,

Detroit, or even Cincinnati. There were no flights to any place from which she might rent a car and drive to Evanston. She was stuck in New York for the night, and it even looked like she was not going to get home in time for tomorrow's investor meeting.

It was the wrong time to be letting the rest of the executive team down. She sat down in one of the empty terminal chairs and fought to calm herself. There was nothing she could do about this. If they thought she was letting them down, that was their tough luck. And maybe the time to be a team player was slipping away anyway.

Then a thought hit her like a blow. Allen had sent her on this trip because he knew she'd get stuck here. He didn't *want* her at the investors meeting. Was she being paranoid? Did Allen have access to better weather reports than she did?

She got the Web on her phone again and called up the weather site. There was a "history" button. Why the weather site would want to archive old weather reports was a conundrum, but it was useful for something like this. She looked at the weather reports for the previous 2 days and learned they had been predicting the cancellation of flights into O'Hare this evening for some time.

Nia had been foolish not to check the weather reports herself, but she'd been so eager to get to New York to talk with Pierre she hadn't given it a thought. Nevertheless, this was strong evidence Allen had sent her here with the intent that she'd miss the investors meeting. Was there nothing he wouldn't stoop to?

She looked down at the phone in her hand. Maybe she would make some calls.

* * *

Sarbanes-Oxley seemed to weigh disproportionately on Ward. Everyone in his professional community referred to it as SOX legislation, except for one friend—CFO at a software company—who liked to refer to it as "The Auditors' Welfare and Guaranteed Annuity Act." In Ward's experience, the joke masked a grim reality. The government, shareholders, customers—even the firm's own auditors for chrissakes—viewed the directors and executives as rapacious crooks selling shoddy products at inflated prices while pocketing spectacular paychecks. Such was the atmosphere in which Novarum Pharmaceuticals held the quarterly circuses reported in the press as "investors meetings." Fortunately for Ward, his responsibilities consisted of a proforma report on Novarum's financial condition and then simply producing numbers whenever Allen didn't have them immediately at hand.

Still, he always felt a little like he should begin his report with "We who are about to die salute you."

But he didn't. He spoke the prescribed incantations in the prescribed order: "generally accepted accounting principles," "continuing operations," "current environment." The incantations had unfortunately never caused him to vanish before their very eyes, but they did seem to prevent their directing the nastiest questions to him. The nastiest questions were reserved for Allen, which worked out fairly well because, for reasons Ward could never fathom, Allen actually liked these meetings. He seemed to delight in the give and take. Or maybe that was smash and grab.

"While profits are nearly comparable with our competitors," concluded Ward in his best professionally disinterested voice, "revenues remain stubbornly flat and G&A costs are creeping upward. My colleagues will describe actions we are taking to redress the situation." He left the lectern without looking up at anyone.

The other executives followed Ward. The chief operating officer reported on the reorganization and anticipated operational efficiencies due to outsourcing of many staff functions. Dr. Milind Desai, after a longish piece on promising drugs in the pipeline, delivered the news that Ward and the other executives knew was most likely to make the rest of the meeting uncomfortable. "Although not final," said Desai, "the FDA has indicated they will not renew our patent on NovarumRT. We are, of course, appealing the ruling and are hopeful of a reversal on their decision, which we view as seriously in error regarding the unique molecular properties and efficacy of NovarumRT."

Ward did not look up from the notes he pretended to study in his lap, but he could sense a ripple of motion in the audience. It was decorous motion, however: silent, restrained, tense. Ward wondered if the audience weren't gathering themselves to pounce. Is this how the elk feels surrounded by the wolves?

One by one, the officers stepped to the lectern and spun their version of Novarum's quarterly story. But Desai's report was out there, and there seemed as much interest in this part of the proceedings as if the executives had been describing their bowel health. Finally Allen took his place at the lectern, made a few soothing remarks, and opened the floor for questions.

In the macho culture that defines big league investors, the initial questions were relatively mild.

Until the analyst from Birnbaum Yamada Securities weighed in. Ward knew the man from previous meetings as Oscar Miller.

"Allen." Ward had never heard Miller address Allen as "Doctor," despite Allen's skill at establishing his credentials whenever he spoke in public. "Why did you kill the joint venture with Temel Ilac, S.A.? The project had great potential for revenue growth."

"Glad you asked, Oscar," said Allen. "The security risk was too great. After a thorough analysis of their capabilities, we concluded this foreign firm could not comply with Novarum's rigorous standards for data encryption. It was a reluctant conclusion. We looked forward to establishing a partnership with Temel Ilac and spent considerable time with the firm. But we learned from this temporary setback. In fact, this experience sets the foundation for our newly established Global Sales and Marketing division, through which we will explore a variety of opportunities with overseas companies. Next question, please."

"Allen." Miller spoke again before anyone else could. "My sources tell me you demanded that Temel Ilac employ OTP in data communication. It's my understanding that OTP is not only impractical but is in some senses obsolete. Certainly no one else in the pharmaceutical industry uses it. Several of Novarum's competitors do a large volume of business in Europe and the developing world using conventional data security protocols. Why would you scuttle a project with such enormous upside? Especially given the imminent loss of revenue you face when NovarumRT goes off patent. We're talking about losses in the hundreds of millions and a potential drop in share price of thirty to fifty percent. Are you acting in the best interest of Novarum when you stop such an attractive venture because of the remote possibility of a security problem? Temel Ilac is one of the largest and most respected pharmaceutical firms in the Middle East. Aren't you aware of what your competitors are doing in the region?"

Allen started to respond, but Miller continued, hardly pausing.

"For instance, credible sources inform me that Rotare Pharmaceuticals recently formed a joint venture with IndoPharma to supply the Indonesian government with drugs worth hundreds of millions in annual sales. Nary a word about data security in that deal, even though IndoPharma will have appropriate access to Rotare's IT systems. Why should Novarum's leadership be so cautious? Are there other reasons why you broke off the negotiations with Temel Ilac?"

He finally stopped. No one else was speaking. Apparently, they all wanted to hear Allen's response.

"Security first," said Allen. "We can't put our intellectual property at risk, Oscar. Our investors wouldn't stand for it, would they? And, as the COO and I have both stated, we are establishing a new division with the intention of expanding our overseas operations soon."

Miller was apparently not finished yet. The rest of the audience continued to defer to him as he pursued his inquiry.

"Won't that take months, if not years, to find a reliable partner, Allen? Why not pursue the Temel Ilac deal now? Why do you need to spend precious time reorganizing your office? I thought you people had a strategic planning function. Isn't that group responsible for these types of joint ventures? Why bother to form what some might see as a redundant organizational structure? Today's firms need to be flat, not dense."

"This is a new structure to better equip us for the future." Allen smiled, then pointedly looked at someone on the other side of the room.

But Ward could see that Miller had bitten deep. The others were prepared to exploit the wound he'd made.

"The future is now, Dr. Hanna," said another analyst. "Novarum's revenue trend is unacceptable to my investors."

"Dr. Hanna," called out an analyst from Employees Worldwide, a very large pension fund, "my clients are concerned about the job losses that will occur because of your outsourcing scheme. How will these displaced people be treated by Novarum?"

"More to the point, Dr. Hanna," another analyst interjected, "is it advisable to initiate a major outsourcing plan in the middle of labor contract negotiations? All of your manufacturing plants are unionized, as are many of the back offices."

The EW analyst jumped in again, "I'm told Novarum's three main unions are determined to fight management on this one. Why add to Novarum's notoriously poor relations with labor by outsourcing jobs? Is the cost savings worth the risk of a strike or labor unrest?"

"I beg to differ." Allen spoke into the microphone and, being the loudest voice in the room, silenced them for a moment. "We have excellent relations with the unionized staff."

"The facts say otherwise," said a new voice. "Novarum ranks near the bottom on labor grievances and employee opinion surveys. Unlike several big pharma firms, Novarum never shows up on the '100 Best Places to Work' list."

"Besides labor issues, Dr. Hanna," called out a woman, "how can you say on the one hand that you're concerned about data security, and on the other hand outsource functions to India? Doesn't that make Novarum more vulnerable to industrial espionage or sabotage?"

"Not at all. Excelsior Consulting will guarantee IT security," said Allen.

"Then, why not use Excelsior as your IT service bureau and proceed with the Temel Ilac joint venture? Our sources inform us that the project holds great promise."

For once, none of the other executives sprang in to help out, and Ward watched Allen struggle with the rapid-fire questions as if he were Moby Dick, impervious to their harpoons and occasionally lashing out to splinter one of their boats. At last he sounded.

"Novarum Pharmaceuticals is fortunate to have such a concerned, active group of investors, willing to advise us and offer the benefit of their insights. I think it's the mark of an effective manager to learn from others. I've learned a lot here today, and I promise you will see immediate results as we begin to take advantage of your advice. Thank you for coming."

Nobody had any comebacks for that, apparently. The audience gathered their papers among a great deal of mumbling and sidelong glances at Allen and filed out. Allen stood at the podium with what Ward thought must be a case-hardened smile.

The executives did not leave the dais, since they were remaining for the follow-up press conference, a ritual Ward hated even more than the investors meeting. Ward approached Allen, away from the microphones. "Have you decided to reconsider the partnership?"

"Not on your life." Allen spoke softly.

"What about that stuff about learning from them?"

"I did learn from them—that Novarum Pharmaceuticals is partly owned by a bunch of carping kibitzers."

Ward didn't know whether to laugh or flee.

But the reporters were entering, and it seemed prudent to just sit down again.

Allen made a bland statement about global pressures and the hopes he had for Novarum's reorganization, then asked for questions.

"Dr. Hanna," said one of the reporters, "Temel Ilac's CEO informed this reporter that the firm has grave doubts about the fullness of your decision to stop the project from going forward. What do you say to that?"

"This is the United States, not the Middle East. We see things differently here. If Temel Ilac doesn't understand the need for data security, perhaps it's because their culture hasn't fully evolved to our level."

"Is this some kind of code for ethnic inferiority, Dr. Hanna?"

"Not at all. I am saying that they may lack some of the infrastructure necessities that would make for a comfortable partnership."

"Necessities?" another reporter asked.

"Yes, such as contract law versus Sharia, for example. Muslim countries have a very different view of lending and profit making."

"But Turkey is not under Sharia. Furthermore, Temel Ilac has been in business for years, turning substantial profits, and has seven years of unqualified financials from Blackwell Investor Services, International. How can you say the firm isn't business savvy?"

Before Allen could answer, another reporter shouted out his question.

"Dr. Hanna, is it time for Novarum to introduce a new generation of leaders to embrace, rather than simply react to a globalized marketplace?"

That's what distinguished reporters from investors and analysts. The reporters went right for the personality questions.

Allen shrugged off the coarseness of the question and answered as if it were a personal challenge directed at him. "We have over one hundred years of combined leadership at Novarum, and it would be a gift to our competitors to let these talented people go. Novarum doesn't stand outside of the normal business cycle. We will rebound with the same team that gave our investors record profits for many years. Let's not come to hasty conclusions as to the cause of our current challenges."

"But your competitors in the drug industry are flourishing, Dr. Hanna. Are they standing outside the business cycle?"

"Is that question rhetorical?" Allen shot back and called on another.

Another one shouted out a question. It was Oscar Miller again. Was the man a reporter as well as an analyst, or did he just like to make trouble?

"Speaking of leadership," asked Miller, "why is Eleanor Marcus leaving the board? Is her vision for Novarum at odds with yours? Isn't she the member who did the most urging for an Novarum-Temel Ilac joint venture?"

It was uncanny how much this man knew about events at Novarum Pharmaceuticals. He seemed to be as familiar with their struggles as any member of the executive team.

For once, Allen's bland expression faltered. "What are you implying?"

"Is there dissension between you two?"

Allen's face flushed and his hands held the lectern a bit tighter, "I find that question impertinent. Dr. Marcus and I enjoy a collegial relationship. She intends to pursue other professional interests. Her decision to leave Novarum's board after two years of service is voluntary. This is not a reprisal."

"Who said anything about a reprisal?"

Ward could see Allen's grip on the lectern relax as the CEO regained control. "Thank you for attending the meeting, ladies and gentlemen."

Reporters continued to shout questions, but they were shouting at Allen's back.

Instructor's Resources

Learning Goals

Based on reading this chapter and knowledge of leadership and organizational behavior theory, students will be able to

- describe the personality traits most related to behavior under pressure
- describe ways an effective leader behaves when severely challenged.

Discussion Questions and Possible Instructor's Responses

Q1 ***Is Nia's conclusion—that Allen deceptively sent her to NYC to prevent her from returning to Chicago in time to attend the investors meeting—warranted?***

Maybe. At this point, she is assuming the worst in Allen. What prevents her from calling Allen to check out her fears, concerns, and hopes? The situation may be dire for her, but it may not be irreparable.

Q2 ***Assuming Nia has disclosed information to an outsider, is her behavior justified?***

Understandable, yes. Jusitified, no. Further, it is unethical and, quite possibly illegal. From a practical standpoint, it is also a destructive act because Allen will most likely conclude that Nia leaked confidential information.

Q3 ***Is Allen's behavior at the investors meeting unusual? Excessive? Too aggressive? Does he make a plausible argument for cancelling the Temel Ilac deal?***

A bit of defensiveness and haughtiness is not that unusual from CEOs. It becomes a problem when carried to an extreme, as Allen did. Even, indeed especially, under pressure, the CEO role demands composure. The ability to remain calm, optimistic, and reassuring is a basic competency of leadership that separates the effective from the ineffective executive. Spectacular derailments have occurred in these situations, as when Enron's CEO Jeff Skilling publicly swore at a stock analyst. Skilling's outburst motivated the business press to scrutinize Enron's questionable accounting practices, leading to the firm's bankruptcy and prison sentences for several of its executives.

Q4 ***At what point does Allen's professional bearing falter, and why?***

Suggesting Middle Eastern countries "lack necessities" for international capitalism. Here, he goes too far.

Q5 ***Is Allen the victim of political correctness?***

Maybe, in the sense that the press can easily use this phrase "lack necessities" as a soundbite to sensationalize Allen's remarks and label him as ethnocentric and retrograde. Still, he is engaging in stereotypic thinking by lumping all Eastern countries together. The amount of diversity within the Islamic nations is substantial, as is their proven ability to conduct responsible, effective, and successful business at home and abroad.

8

Damaged Goods

Stuck on the tarmac at Kennedy, Nia wondered if there would be any fallout from her phone calls the evening before. She would find out soon enough when she got back to the office.

The flight attendant came on the p.a. system and said the captain gave permission for passengers to use their communication devices as long as the aircraft was waiting for takeoff, which looked like it might some time yet. Nia took her Blackberry out of her bag, started it up, and checked her e-mail. In a short time, she had a long list of messages on the little screen. Scrolling through them, she was startled to read the subject "Congratulations" on a message sent by Allen.

The news was even more startling. She read the text three times, parsing the message more carefully with each reading. The conclusion was inescapable: she was being moved aside under the pretext of a promotion carrying a 20% raise and a nebulous title that retained her executive status and not much else. Allen was creating a new unit—Global Sales and Marketing—which would hollow out her department. And she was not being considered to run it.

The Varieties of Leadership at Novarum Pharmaceuticals: A Novel, pages 129–140

Jack Welch wrote an article about this kind of move, which he called "dead man walking." Better to fire the person than kick them upstairs, was Neutron Jack's advice. The new EVP of Global Sales and Marketing would undoubtedly command a bigger salary. A man? Probably.

Eventually the plane got off the ground and she had to put the Blackberry away. She seethed quietly for the entire flight.

Once the plane landed and she disembarked, she went directly from the gate to find a newsstand and get a paper. The account of Novarum's quarterly report was not pleasant. The reporter, who clearly didn't believe her flight had been cancelled so that she'd been forced to spend the night in New York, had taken her absence from the meeting as evidence she was a casualty of Allen's announced reorganization. She knew the truth, but she felt embarrassed as she read the article.

As she trudged to the baggage pick-up, she realized she had not switched the Blackberry back on. When she did, it rang almost immediately to notify her of her voice messages.

Jenna had left two messages from her cell phone in the last 90 minutes. Nia pressed "call back."

Jenna answered before the completion of the first ring.

"Nia! Have you heard what's happened?"

Assuming Jenna was referring to Allen's e-mail, but not certain if it was public knowledge, she tried to be noncommittal.

"I read in the paper that yesterday's investor meeting didn't go well," she said.

Jenna didn't even acknowledge this but launched right into her story. "Maldonado," she sniffed.

Was she crying? Nia remembered Maldonado as VP of HR—an aloof guy who never bothers to chat with the cubicle dwellers. "What about him, Jenna? Are you OK?"

"I'm sorry." Jenna sniffed again. "I'm just so mad. I've been sitting here going over it and over it and I guess I've worked myself into a state."

"What is it? What did he do?"

"He came into my office first thing this morning." Jenna sniffed again. When she spoke again, her voice seemed to have regained its composure. "He came into my office first thing morning with a security guard. They gave me fifteen minutes to gather my personal belongings, and the guard 'escorted' me off the Novarum campus. I'm in my car, parked on a goddamn street in Evanston. I'm fired."

"Good God." Nia wondered if she were somehow connected to this. "Why?"

"You tell me. The official reason is Novarum is outsourcing staff functions as part of a cost containment push. Apparently other staff functions are being outsourced as well."

"This is . . ." Nia searched for a word, came up with nothing. ". . . bad." It was the only thing she could think of.

"Tell me about it. I should have gotten suspicious when I saw the Excelsior people slinking around the executive suite."

"Excelsior Consulting?" Last week, three men had left Allen's office while she was in the waiting room. By their demeanor, she had taken them for ordinary sales guys. She should have recognized the uniform. They'd had working buttons on their jacket cuffs. Bespoke suits.

"You got it. You know their pitch. They stoke fear, greed, and ego. 'If you have the courage to control costs, you can strengthen your company's competitive position. And, oh, by the way, expect a nice spike in your share price next quarter.'"

"You seem to know how these people work," said Nia.

Jenna hesitated before responding: "Actually, I was a key member of the outsourcing committee at Axton Pharmaceuticals. We used the consultants from RamSys, but I'm sure the script is the same with Excelsior. I left AP soon after the outsourcing was completed, in part because I felt tainted by what I helped to implement. We cut payroll by fifteen percent—actual jobs, not just unfilled positions—in a firm that had an annual ROI of over twenty percent for the past decade. Axton had patents on two blockbusters. The combined executive take was in the hundreds of millions when the stock shot up. Perfectly legal, of course. But bare knuckled capitalism."

"What now? Severance pay, career services . . . ?" Nia's voice trailed off.

"The package is good. I can't gripe about that. But I'm furious and humiliated. I've given a lot to Novarum: good corporate citizen, active in the HR community, and exemplary performance appraisals. I hired scores of people at Novarum over the past eight years, and I always found good things to say about the mission and culture."

"Yeah," said Nia. "like a family, right?"

Jenna laughed bitterly.

"Jenna, how many people from HR were let go this morning?"

"You mean kicked out? We're all let go. But only three of us were kicked out. Everyone else is allowed to close out over the next three months or so. That's why I'm humiliated. I have much more seniority than the other two supervisors they fired this morning. I don't know why I got singled out for the security-escort treatment."

Nia recalled the heated conversation about compensation she had with Allen, but decided not to share it with Jenna. No sense in upsetting her further.

"Jenna, how can I help? Reference? Contacts?"

Should she offer to appeal to Allen?

"Thanks, Nia. Nothing at the moment. I'm in shock right now. I need to lick my wounds before starting the odious process of searching for a job. But I'm guardedly optimistic that I can get one. I have HR contacts, after all. And after the AP experience, I resolved to never again get psychologically hooked on a corporation. Even one with a family feeling."

"Words to live by," said Nia. "While you're regaining your balance, don't isolate yourself. Maybe I and others can help you through this period. In fact, are you up for biking the Lake Michigan trail Saturday morning?"

"Short or long?"

"Jenna, when did we ever do the short trail?"

"Actually, never. See you Saturday at ten a.m."

Rather than catching a cab, Nia returned to O'Hare's newly constructed meditation chapel. In the post-9/11 world, air travelers need all the help they can get. She wasn't actually the victim of a terrorist attack, but she might as well have been.

* * *

Pierre had spent the morning soothing clients and had not yet had a chance to do any of the database searching he'd wanted to get done before lunch. He felt troubled, and that feeling was compounded by a call from Nia. But he knew if he put her off, he would just have to deal with her later. Besides, she deserved to be treated professionally and with respect. He put on a smile and greeted her as if she could see it.

"How nice to hear from you."

"Same here. How are you, Pierre?"

Was that the edge of tension in her voice?

"Harried, actually. Terribly sorry I couldn't return your phone calls. After we met, I was promoted to director of the East Coast client services. My workload has tripled." He sighed theatrically. "Now, if only my salary would keep pace."

"Congratulations, Pierre. I'm sure it's well deserved."

Pierre was dreading the rest of the conversation, but for him, every conversation went through three phases: small talk, intelligence gathering, and the business at hand. He thanked her for the congratulations and decided it was time to move on to phase two. "How is Dr. Marcus?"

"Pierre, do you actually know everyone in health care management, or does it just seem that way?"

Pierre laughed. "I've been thinking about her lately."

"She's fine, Pierre. Looking forward to ridding humanity of the scourge of ulcers."

"Ah, yes. Rotare, isn't it? And she'll be working on Marshal's team with Finosec?"

"You do know everybody!"

"I must send her a note. Do you have her forwarding address?"

"Yes, I'll send you her contact information."

"And what about you, Nia? How are you faring these days?"

"I'm fine. Of course, as you might have guessed, my search for a new position has heated up."

"So I've gathered."

"To get right to the point: I have carefully considered the two positions we discussed. I'm especially interested in the CAO role and would like to explore it further."

"Ah, yes. So . . ." Pierre could hear himself hesitating. He knew he didn't sound as if he were in control, but he couldn't think of any other way to handle this—not if he was going to be honest with her. "The thing is, Nia, the CAO position isn't quite open at this time."

"You mean your client cancelled the search? Why?"

"Not exactly cancelled."

"Please continue."

"The firm in question is deeply conservative. Nonprofit with heavy financial support from a highly ethical foundation. Pillar of the community and all that. They shy away, no, sprint away from controversy."

There was a brief silence at the other end of the line.

"Nia? Hello?"

"I'm controversial?"

"I'm afraid so."

She didn't protest, and Pierre thought with relief the conversation would soon be over.

"Very well, then," she said. "The other EVP position was also attractive. The learning curve for a lateral within big pharma won't be very steep, and I would like to return to the East Coast. It could be fun. Let's put my name forward for that position. You mentioned they are eager to get someone on board ASAP. I've moved into the eager category too."

"I'm afraid that isn't an option at this time, either."

"Why not?" said Nia. "What controversy are they afraid of?"

"Umm . . ." Pierre was disgusted with himself for peppering his conversation with nonwords. Why couldn't he just say it? "Actually, Nia, right now you are . . ." He hesitated again. "I guess the term is 'radioactive.'"

"Me? Personally?"

Pierre took a deep breath and continued.

"It's unusual for an executive to leave a company after two years. Either the person failed to investigate the position sufficiently to determine goodness of fit between her skills and the job's requirements—a lack of intelligence, perhaps. Or, once aboard didn't work well with others—a people problem. Neither trait is desirable, but the former is much easier to explain to a prospective employer than the latter."

"My strategic thinking skills are beyond reproach. Are you questioning my conceptual abilities?"

"No. Not at all."

"Then what are you questioning?"

"What distinguishes executives from those who don't climb to the top? It's rarely intellectual horsepower. Rather, it's more often lack of flexibility and political dexterity."

"Political dexterity?"

"Yes. Starting with an accurate accounting of one's facts, figures, and friends, knowing when to compromise, when to accommodate, and when to push back. Further, knowing how to do that in a way that saves face for every actor on the stage."

"Then you're implying—concluding really, from one work experience—that I don't play well with others?"

"Maybe you didn't play well with the one person who counted most."

"Please let me understand you, Pierre. You're saying because I advocated for a different strategic direction than my boss—a very well-reasoned direction, I might add—that I'm now, what... damaged goods?"

"That's far too harsh an assessment, Nia. You've had an impressive career thus far. However, the public nature of Novarum's leadership difficulties makes placing anyone from the executive team a delicate case at the moment."

"Won't people see that I'm leaving a company that's going in the wrong direction?"

"Nia, names came up in public meetings. People watching this political drama may come to some well-founded conclusions."

"Who might be watching, Pierre?"

"Me. My current and future clients. Industry insiders."

"And what are your—their—conclusions?"

Pierre could imagine her at the other end of the line. He didn't think she'd be crying, but he knew she would probably wince at the next remark. Nevertheless, there was no help for it. "Oscar Miller knew too much about what has been going on at Novarum. He didn't get his information from Eleanor Marcus, and he didn't get it from any of the executives who were at the investors meeting. That leaves only one person who might have washed Novarum laundry in public."

* * *

Reynold leaned back in the chair and looked at Allen across the little bistro table. "You're normally not this easy to beat, old sport. What's wrong? Didn't have time for your pregame double macchiato?"

"Cute," said Allen.

Reynold recognized he was trying to cut him off, but he wasn't going to let his friend off the hook. He continued as if Allen hadn't said anything.

"Normally you're an aggressive server. I kept waiting for the attack, assuming your weak serves were something of a feint."

Allen sighed.

Reynold stopped talking and waited for a response.

"I'm not in much of an attack mode right now." Allen played with his bottled water.

Reynold knew exactly what was eating him, but he felt he could be a better friend by feigning ignorance. "Anything wrong?"

Allen didn't look up from the paper label he'd begun to peel off his bottle with his thumbnail. "Problems at work, I guess."

"Want to talk about them?"

Allen looked up. "No."

Reynold decided some competitive sparring might cheer him up.

"Well, even if you were in an attack mode," he said, "I could still hand you your shirt."

Allen looked down at the bottle and began to worry its label again. "You don't always win."

"Only when I want to."

Allen looked up. Taking an interest?

"What do you mean by that?"

"I decide most of our games." He kept his voice light, but he knew there was some truth to what he was saying.

"Bullshit," said Allen.

"Oh, I don't decide them by myself," said Reynold. "I do it by reading you."

Allen just nodded for him to continue.

"Your flash point is rather low, once someone gets your number. Most people don't probe to find it because of your credentials and bearing. Especially now that you're the *queso grande* at NP. But I know some of your soft spots. Besides, you're not writing my performance appraisal, so where's the risk? When we're playing, I say little things that irritate you and, in the aggregate, cause you to lose your concentration. Then you push hard, relying on aggression without sufficient strategy. You know the neuroscience behind thought and emotion. Emotion has a nasty habit of winning out over rationality. Our primitive brain kicks in and we lash out. You're not a hothead. But you are provokable."

"Thanks for the pyschoanalysis."

He was being sarcastic and Reynold knew it. "I'm a sports-medicine practitioner. There aren't many fields in which psychology is more important."

"Maybe you should save the psychology for your sports-medicine patients."

"You're feeling pretty low, aren't you?"

Allen shrugged as if feeling low didn't bother him. But Reynold could tell by the forward tilt of his head and the sag of his shoulders that it was a pose.

"Come on," said Reynold. "This is Reynold you're talking to."

Allen exhaled noisily. "My job's on the line. The Board is meeting tomorrow in a special session. I wasn't supposed to know about the meeting but my secretary accidentally told me about it. She was clearly upset with herself for the slip up. And worried too, I think, that she broke confidences with whoever pledged her to secrecy. I was in no mood to allay her fear."

Reynold leaned across the table, feeling like he didn't want to miss a word.

The woman they had talked about last time, Nia, played a starring role in Allen's brief story. But now it also had rebellious investors, snarky reporters, dirty linen aired in public, and a Turkish company that seemed to feel it had been jilted. The strain in Allen's voice and face was apparent, and rather than being relieved by getting it off his chest, he seemed to grow more resentful and self-justifying as the story developed. "Now I could find myself out of a job, and it's all because I tried to do right by our shareholders."

Neither man spoke for a minute. Reynold didn't know whether to respond as a friend, an advisor, or Allen's physician. Maybe he could do all three by choreographing some humor.

"Allen, how did this happen?" he said at last.

"Are you listening? I just told you how this happened. I was blindsided by an ambitious subordinate and her accomplice. Didn't you know that sisterhood is powerful?"

"Are there other ways to look at this situation?"

"Are you pulling a 'clinical' on me, Reynold? Trying to get me to see it your way by that using that tiresome counseling technique?"

"You sound angry, Allen."

They both laughed at the transparency of what every Psych 101 student is taught about paraphrasing and labeling feelings.

Tension lessened a bit.

"Why don't you tell me what you think." said Allen.

"Really? You want me to be frank?"

"Of course. For God's sake, Reynold. We're not in middle school."

"Okay, relax." Reynold took a breath as if getting ready to dive in. "I didn't like the sound of this from the start. You could have handled Nia's challenge about her compensation in many ways. You didn't have to lie."

Allen started to protest.

Reynold held up his hand. "Please let me speak."

Allen sat back against his chair again.

"That deception may have set this whole situation—mess, really—in motion. You don't know what Nia did behind your back, if anything. But is it a fair assumption that she was enraged when you tried to nix the proposal, lie about her compensation, and impugn her motives?"

"This is business. We all have to live with disappointments."

Reynold continued. "Anger is not on the same plane as disappointment. Disappoint dissipates. That's what Friday night happy hour is for. Anger lingers. Festers."

"All right, so she's angry. Does that justify her despicable actions?"

"Maybe she didn't speak to Eleanor, and maybe she never heard of that Wall Street analyst. But what if she had?"

"Then she went over my head and around my back. It's wrong!"

"And what if her methods were wrong but her goals were right? From my knowledge of Novarum's position in the industry, I think she put forth a very attractive proposal that you should have approved."

"And data security? What about that, Reynold? Would you want to risk your money in a joint venture with a firm that might be penetrated by terrorists?"

"As a matter of fact, Allen, I own a substantial number of Rotare shares. My broker e-mailed me this morning recommending I increase my holdings in the firm on the announcement of a likely joint venture between Rotare and a certain Turkish firm."

Allen was stunned.

"You're investing in Rotare?"

"Allen, why are you so shocked? It is just business. You said so yourself."

Instructor's Resources

Learning Goals

Based on reading this chapter and knowledge of leadership and organizational behavior theory, students will be able to

- describe the ethical responsibility that friends have to each other in a work organization
- describe the ethical responsibility that subordinates have to their superiors
- evaluate the appropriateness and likely consequences of disclosing confidential information to those with a questionable right to know
- continue the conversation about the consequences of unethical behavior for followers and leaders

Discussion Questions and Possible Instructor's Responses

Q1 *Is Jenna's termination a reprisal from Allen?*

Probably. She may have leaked salary information to her friend Nia. Of course, Allen can't know that for sure, so his action is irresponsible.

Q**2** ***Should Nia have told Jenna about her confrontation with Allen in which she discussed her perceived salary inequities?***

Debatable. It wouldn't change the outcome for Jenna, and it would probably damage Nia's friendship with Jenna, possibly permanently. Plus, to our knowledge, Jenna was not forced to share confidential information with Nia. Whoever discloses confidential information runs the risk that the information will be shared with others, possibly with attribution. We can't assume Jenna, as a corporate citizen, is naïve to this fact of life. But her unauthorized disclosure of confidential information contributes to a disastrous outcome for the principals, including the hundreds of Novarum employees who are losing their jobs.

Q**3** ***Should Nia have been surprised by what happens in Pierre's office?***

A rational, disinterested observer wouldn't be surprised at the outcome. Nia acted out of anger and a desire for revenge. Had she stopped and sought counsel from Eleanor or others, she probably would not have behaved in such a destructive way.

Pierre is acting in a prudent fashion. Were he compassionate, he might offer her advice and the hope of recovering from her errors. Even if he isn't compassionate, it is sound business practice to help an executive in need. Nia would be unlikely to forget his assistance, and we can conclude that she will recover from this career setback.

Q**4** ***Are you surprised that Allen's secretary is not loyal?***

No. Self-interest is the foundation of business relationships. Allen probably expects too much from others, i.e., loyalty. Anger is often an emotional reaction to an ethical breach. That is, we experience anger when others don't live up to our expectations of proper, fair behavior. In this respect, Allen and Nia are angry with each other for the same reason: a violation of the fairness principle. This leads both of them to engage in self-justifying acts that benefit, in the end, neither themselves, Novarum employees, nor investors.

Q**5** ***Is Reynold's assessment of the situation accurate?***

Yes, this story is Allen's undoing of himself. His inability to control his emotions and a deeply competitive nature, combined with a lack of checks and balances from the board and his executive team. Allen reacts in a dysfunctional fashion that causes missed opportunities for Novarum and a possible derailment of his career at Novarum, and elsewhere.

Epilogue: Steadfast or Stubborn?

Every corporation, from the largest to the smallest, has four levels. The lowest level is the working level. This the level where the organization's day-to-day work gets accomplished. It encompasses the largest part of the company. Next up from that is the management level. People in this level often participate in the work, but usually their salary is determined by how much they direct the work of the people below them. They are responsible for turning the strategy created by the people in the level above into actions. Directly above the management level is the executive level. These are the people who create the strategy that is implemented by the management level. These people can be considerably separated from the organization's actual work. And above the executive level is one that is probably best characterized as the *ironic* level. That's the Board of Directors.

The irony is that of accountability without control. The employees who actually perform or manage the corporation's work are inevitably protected from serious risk by their status as subordinates. Unless they do something they know is illegal, they can nearly always seek shelter behind a boss. The Directors, on the other hand, though they may have nothing whatever to do with the corporation's day-to-day work, have no such shelter. They can be sued or even prosecuted for the behavior of the corporation. They all know this. The intelligent ones prefer to stay out of jail, and therefore they take their obligations seriously. This means they can't afford to be governed by personal feelings. When a CEO is out of control, they must step in. They may all have been appointed to their directorships by that same CEO, but

The Varieties of Leadership at Novarum Pharmaceuticals: A Novel, pages 141–150

sometimes your own survival means voting somebody off the island, even if you owe him.

Other than the mandatory quarterly meeting, the Novarum Board of Directors did their work by e-mail, and it was unusual for them to meet as a body. But these were unusual times. They met in a conference room at the headquarters of the Pharmaceutical Research and Manufacturers of America (PhRMA), the national trade association of drug companies, in Washington, DC. The board needed some place to meet that wasn't Novarum territory. One of the directors had been an executive at PhRMA, and he had asked for the space from his former colleagues, who were glad to allow it since the conference room wasn't in use that day. Everyone was there but Allen Hanna, who was the question they were trying to decide.

A business meeting that takes up a for-and-against question often resembles Homeric combat. Lots of people stand on the sidelines while two champions meet on the field to contest the question. Those on the sidelines may have feelings about the outcome, but they are mostly there to observe the outcome and to learn which army will have to abandon the field. That's why this meeting was mostly a discussion among three of the seven people in attendance.

Fran Rasmussen struggled to stick to the facts and not let her impatience creep into what she was saying. She was impatient with people who didn't measure up, especially those she expected the most from—especially those who refused to entertain doubts about themselves. She could not abide smugness. It was an attitude she developed at a residential private school she had attended as a teenager. It was one of the most exclusive private schools on the American east coast. The girls around her were smug, although heaven knows few of them had any personal qualities that warranted it. They just had money, the possession of which often turns into a sense of entitlement. Allen Hanna reminded her of some of the insufferable girls she went to school with.

"He hasn't gotten in front of the story," she said. "He's so convinced of his own righteousness he keeps digging his hole deeper."

A couple others at the table nodded.

She continued. "In both of the public appearances since that investors' assault, Allen's displayed a superior, maybe even angry posture. He's disregarded our numerous suggestions for righting the ship. Is he oblivious to the seriousness of this? Forgetting substance for a moment, it's become a PR disaster. Sad, really. Allen was a smart guy, a talented guy."

"He still is a talented guy," said Chris Tabor. "Let's be clear. The FDA ruling was wrong and unfair. The stock is, therefore, being battered. Allen's a physician, not an alchemist. Can he be expected to transform Novarum's loss of a prime revenue source into a tale of gold?"

Chris was the newest member of the board of directors and seemed intent on proving himself stupid. But Fran refused to be smug.

"I'm not sure about the analogy, Chris, but I get your point," she said. "Of course the FDA ruling was unfair. We all know that."

So the meeting had hardly started and the ground was staked out. It was going to be Fran versus Chris. In the struggle, Fran's assets would be seniority, experience, and realism. Chris's would be the enthusiasm, a fresh point of view, and the board's reluctance. Nobody likes to make hard decisions, even those who are paid handsomely to do it.

"Why didn't he emphasize our contributions to the communities we've operated in for the past fifty years?" said Dana Redman, who apparently took the side of reluctance. "Or the savings of ethical drugs compared to the cost of hospitalization? For instance, the total cost of full hip surgery can run as high as forty-thousand dollars. By contrast, the cost of a year's worth of preventive medicine costs approximately one-thousand dollars."

Redman had come to the board from the industry association. He was, in other words, a lobbyist. Few took him seriously.

Fran still didn't want to be smug. But she didn't want to waste time, either.

"Are we digressing?" she said pointedly.

Redman shrank back in his chair. "Sorry," he mumbled.

"Now, then," continued Fran. "Today's agenda concerns Allen's handling of issues that a CEO should be able to influence."

She looked around the table. Nobody protested. It was apparent to everyone, reluctance or not, that Allen had let a difficult situation grow into a PR disaster.

"Maybe the stress is affecting him," said Chris.

Fran was pleased she'd got a concession from him already, so she zeroed in on it quickly. "His communication style and logic both seem to have eluded him. How could he possibly make public remarks that sounded to some people like invidious comparison between U.S. and Middle Eastern business practices?"

"*Some*? You mean a *lot* of people, don't you?" said Redman, who had determined the direction of the prevailing wind and decided to throw his lot in with Fran.

"But I disagree that stress is causing Allen to misspeak," she said. "His comments are intentional, and he's very confident in his reasoning. Determinedly so. Even smug." She looked around the table, daring anyone to disagree. No one did.

"I think he resents being called to account for these decisions," she continued. "He's had an unblemished career. My sense is Dr. Hanna isn't accustomed to this level of scrutiny, especially in public. People are questioning his rationale and competence."

"And honesty?" said Dana.

"I agree with Fran," said Chris. "He doesn't know how to say 'I've made some mistakes, and here's what I intend to do to correct them.' We've even given him the script. The last press conference he conducted was feeble, as in 'If mistakes were made, I bear the ultimate responsibility.' Such self-defensive, egotistical . . ." His voice trailed off.

"Allen bristles at having to read from someone else's script," said Fran. "That's why his statement was evasive and in the past tense. Besides, he doesn't think he has anything to apologize for."

"By the way, why did Eleanor recuse herself from this meeting?" asked Chris, who knew Eleanor Marcus as a frequent ally.

"Her term is expiring very soon, and she thought it inappropriate to offer a judgment on the future of Novarum so close to her departure," said Fran.

"Of course I know that," said Chris. "I'm asking, what is the real reason she's not here today? Is there some truth to Miller's allegation of bad blood between her and Allen? I've never detected a bit of it, I must say."

"I thought their relationship went back many years," said Dana. "Allen trusted Eleanor. He hired Nia Stevens based on Eleanor's recommendation."

"Listen, folks." Fran betrayed a little of her impatience. "Eleanor doesn't matter at this point. Furthermore, Nia agreed to resign without protest. The office of general counsel is drafting her separation package as we speak."

"I for one, would like to see her depart the premises today," said Chris, who felt Nia was the source of Allen's current problems. "I will not approve that woman's separation agreement if it says anything positive about her performance at Novarum."

"Understood," said Dana. "The announcement will be noncommittal, and she will not receive a recommendation. She will be gone soon enough. In the meantime we must guard against another *Wall Street Journal* story on suspected employee reprisals."

"Reprisal?" said Chris. "How about justice for conduct unbecoming an officer?"

"Do we have proof Nia was the one that gave the information to Oscar Miller?" said Fran.

"My people couldn't find any," said Dana. "In the absence of evidence, we can't charge her with a breach of confidentiality."

"Fine, we don't. No matter. That's not where we need to focus our attention, anyway," said Fran. "The urgent matter before us is damage control. For one, how are we going to convincingly explain to our investors that Rotare Pharmaceuticals—surely the most risk-adverse firm in the industry—has entered into joint venture discussions with Temel Ilac? How did this Turkish firm transmute itself from terrorist hotbed to valued foreign partner overnight? I don't think that's alchemy."

"Indeed, how?" asked Dana. "The question got raised and answered all over the business press last week." Owing to his background, he probably read the business press closer than any of the others.

"Then there's the matter of the union locals," said Fran. "Wolinski's managed to galvanize the troops. In total, the locals have filed forty-eight unfair labor practices complaints in the two weeks following Novarum's outsourcing announcement."

"They're trivial and won't stick," said Dana. "Everyone knows they're proxies for anger about Novarum's rightsizing. Thank God employment at-will remains the law of the land. The decision to reduce staff is management's call. But to me, what's more worrisome is how effectively the union's actions attracted the attention of the DNC. Two House members and the Left's iconic senator held a press conference on outsourcing—they never refer to it as rightsizing, by the way—citing Novarum as the most recent evidence of America's race to the bottom."

"What did they allege, Dana?"

"The standard litany: foreign outsourcing eventually depresses wages at home, fails to pay a living wage in the host country, uses child labor, requires employees to work in unsafe and unhealthy facilities, and degrades the environment because the factories have minimal pollution controls."

"Is that all they're complaining about?" Chris looked around expectantly.

Nobody laughed.

"It goes beyond the Hill, though," said Chris. "The PR department is tracking a flurry of blogs, podcasts, newspaper editorials, and talk radio. Not to mention the six o'clock TV. Tearful employees talking to a reporter while standing in front of a Novarum building is not a pretty sight. I remind you all this is happening on our watch."

Everyone nodded. They knew that with this kind of publicity, they were a hair's breadth from one or more shareholder lawsuits. They could all be in line for some unwelcome court experience, not to mention a substantial reduction in their personal fortunes when Novarum Pharmaceuticals' shares descended to the basement.

Fran attempted to summarize. "I think I speak for all of us when I say it's inaccurate to blame one person for the problems of a large organization. Still, Dr. Hanna is the CEO and his handling of the situation, combined with the FDA ruling, is troubling the investor community. His refusal to change course is seen by many as stubbornness, not steadfastness. The recent press conferences exacerbated a somewhat sticky situation. Yes, the failure to consummate the overseas partnership, stimulating union unrest by outsourcing jobs, and not renewing Eleanor's term are issues worthy of debate. But it seems Allen's turned these issues into a crisis for Novarum. As we all know, the leader's job is to frame a situation in such a way that the public buys the company's worldview. At present few are buying Novarum, figuratively, or literally."

"Should we speak with Allen again?" said Chris.

"And say what?"

"An ultimatum?" inquired Dana.

"How about hearing testimony first," said Chris, still grasping at straws.

"Testimony?" said Dana. "We're not the district attorney's office, and Allen's not a criminal. He's made some errors, especially in timing, but that's insufficient reason to bring him down. If we remove Allen now, it is a tacit admission of our own lack of strategic imagination. I say, let's keep Allen out of the public's eye for a while and mount a PR campaign. The furor will abate once Eleanor sets up shop at Rotare, the stock price rallies, and the union settles down. Have a heart-to-heart talk with the man, for goodness sake. He's not that inflexible."

He scanned the room, looking for support from a group of seasoned executives skilled at not disclosing their hands.

The majority of the board had been silent through the discussion. They were hard to read, either because they hadn't made up their minds or they didn't want to be aligned with a losing position.

"Well then, has it gone beyond, uh, coaching Allen?" asked Dana.

"If it has, who will fill the position? Even as acting?"

Silence.

"Maybe Ward Alexander?" said Chris. "CFO. Years of experience. Not impulsive. The street always likes a numbers guy."

"Alexander?" said Fran with irritation. "Wasn't he part of Allen's design team that created the mess we're struggling to extricate ourselves from? He even hired the IT director, Rasheed . . . uhh, how do you pronounce his last name?"

"Rasheed Madhdabi," Chris said. "Ward told me he had good reasons for hiring him. Rasheed is as good as most CIOs, few of whom have ever had to cope with something like this. It's too bad he wasn't up to it."

"How so," asked Dana.

"Evidently Rasheed supported Allen's recommendation of using OTP. He green-lighted Allen's scheme and convinced Ward that it was an acceptable way to exchange information between Novarum and Temel Ilac. Ward was worried about Rasheed's judgment when he got some negative intelligence from a respected member of Rasheed's team, but he figured the guy must know what he's talking about. Rasheed never voiced any serious concerns about the appropriateness of what we now know is an antiquated method. It was only later when the protocol was derided in the computer press did Rasheed back off. Apparently his IT team revolted at that point and, in effect, wrote a letter of no confidence. They even met with Ward at his house to express their dissatisfaction. A few of his long-serving top managers hinted at resigning if something wasn't done. That may have been posturing, of course. According to them, Rasheed was an authoritarian. Maybe it's in his culture to give orders and he misread the collegial culture of Novarum. In the end, Ward had no choice but to fire him. I know this was hard for Ward to get rid of a direct report, but I must say I liked the decisive way he cuts losses." Having delivered his speech, Chris relaxed back into his chair and looked around at the others.

"Ward told me all about the Rasheed situation during a heart-to-heart conversation." said Dana. "At his request, I met with Ward after Allen's awful investors meeting. Speaking in confidence, Ward told me he was an early and consistent supporter of the Temel Ilac joint venture. In fact, he helped Nia more fully develop the projected ROI as a way to bolster her case. He showed me the financials. Impressive work. In a private meeting, he tried to convince Allen to go forward with the project. Allen rejected the plan. Then he abruptly reversed himself for reasons Ward never understood. Of course that reversal didn't stand, even though Ward told me he tried very hard to overcome Allen's concerns about data security. Obviously OTP, the solution Allen somehow hit upon, with Rasheed's support, was the wrong approach. In all of this, Ward was in the middle, trying to find a good solution and trying to keep Allen from going off a pier. Allen would hear none of it."

"It's the first I've heard of this," said Fran. "Why didn't Ward inform us of all this drama?"

"I asked him that," said Dana. "He said it would be improper to go over Allen's head. Especially after Allen swore him to secrecy when he informed Ward of the reorganization and outsourcing plan. Ward thought Allen had gone way too far with those moves and again vigorously argued against the plan, but it was apparent to him that Allen was not asking for his opinion. Allen was determined to drive these changes through. I think Ward only spoke to me because of my reputation for political savvy."

"Can anyone corroborate Ward's rendering of the situation," asked Fran.

No one answered.

"Ward is an impressive guy, in a quiet sort of way," said Chris. "It took some courage for him to share his concerns with Dana."

"True," said Dana. "He does have a command of the numbers. And he doesn't rattle easily. His performance at the investors meeting was very steady, especially compared to Allen's. Sounds like he had good intuition with the IT flap as well."

"Ward will be associated with the old guard," said Fran. "Do we think he's capable of making the changes that need to be made?"

"If you ask me," said Chris, "Ward's best recommendation is his availability. We need to do something fast. The investors aren't going to ride this one out, and they aren't going to give us much time."

"Are we looking for a corporate savior?" asked Fran. "Does such a leader exist?"

A few members appeared to nod in agreement, but it wasn't clear whom they were agreeing with.

"Bearing in mind that our hides are on the line in this too, are we ready to vote?" asked Dana.

A new voice spoke up.

"I think not, Dana."

It was Tom Rafferty. He was the most senior member of the board, and the only one whose tenure predated Allen's. He was, in a sense, the only board member with no reason to be loyal to Allen. But that might have been because Allen was so loyal to him, having kept him on for three term expirations—the only director he'd ever kept beyond a single term.

"Why not, Tom?" said Fran.

"I'm uncomfortable with where this is headed. Frankly it seems a little too . . . tidy. Allen's out and Ward is in. I need more data before voting. I move that we postpone the vote. I will speak with Allen, Eleanor, and whoever else has relevant information." Tom looked around the room. "With all due respect to Ward and his supporters, whenever I've seen an individual emerge from an organizational crisis wearing clean socks, he has always turned out to be someone to regard skeptically. A magician doesn't really make the coin disappear; he just distracts us while he hides it."

"How much time do you need, Tom?"

"Two days. Maybe three."

"I will help, Tom," said Fran. "Frankly I'm a bit dubious about Ward's involvement in all this."

"Me too," said Chris.

"I hear a motion to postpone the vote until, what, two days?" asked Dana. "All in favor, say yea."

The motion carried five to two, and the board adjourned.

* * *

"Thanks for supporting me folks," said Tom after the three stayed behind to decide on an approach to the delicate assignment before them. "Allen's a good friend of mine, but I am prepared to let the facts go where they may."

"Understood," said Fran. "I think we risk compounding the error by removing Allen without a more thorough investigation. I don't like the fact that people are disappearing: Eleanor, Nia, Rasheed."

"Nor do I," said Chris. "Then again, I was never in support of the outsourcing part of Allen's plan. We have hundreds of Novarum employees disappearing. Can that be good for morale? Who's looking out for them?"

"We're supposed to," said Fran with a sigh.

"Do we need to reopen all of the policy calls that brought us to today?" asked Tom. "I'm worried about scope creep."

"I'm worried too, but I think we need a much deeper understanding of how Novarum is being managed. In fact, I want to speak with Nia as well," said Fran.

"Agreed," said Tom. "May I suggest a division of labor?"

"Even though it's more work, I would prefer that we interview every person as a team. I think we need to hear the same story at the same time," said Fran. "And let's cast a wide net. I'm interested in hearing from some of the outsourced HR managers. I received an anonymous e-mail from someone suggesting that the outsourcing plan was designed to punish the HR shop. The message seemed to me to be more the rant of a disgruntled employee, but perhaps there's something to the story."

"Should we speak with the IT team as well?" asked Chris. "Why did they go around their director? What did Ward do with the data? He evidently accepted it as fact and fired Rasheed. Was that precipitous? I think we should speak with the IT team as well. I want to hear more about their relationship with Rasheed and their position on OTP."

"I'm with you on that, Chris," said Tom. "I attended a briefing Rasheed gave, and he struck me as charming, cooperative, and extremely intelligent. It's hard for me to view him as an authoritarian. My gut tells me there is more to this story than the actions of one leader."

"More like a web?" asked Fran.

"Yes. An apt metaphor," said Tom.

A silence descended on them for a moment. Finally Chris spoke up.

"I guess we had better start with a strand and follow it." He opened his laptop. "I have a PowerPoint here that Eleanor Marcus sent me when I talked with her to prepare for this meeting. She says it's a presentation Nia was to give to Allen about the Turkish partnership."

"Let's see it, then," said Fran.

The End

Pharmaceutical Industry: Background[1]

The pharmaceutical industry can be loosely divided into four overlapping categories:

- medical chemical manufacturers who prepare drugs from animal or herb sources and synthesize products into pure form;
- biological product manufacturers who produce vaccines, toxins, and blood serums;
- proprietary product manufacturers who sell over-the-counter, often well-known drugs such as Bayer aspirin;
- private formula [generic] or brand manufacturers who manufacturer prescription-only drugs. These manufacturers are sometimes referred to as "ethical" firms because they supply hospitals and physicians who act as gatekeepers between the firm and the patient.

Approximately 20 corporations in the United States and Europe—Big Pharma—account for 50% of total industry sales. In 2004, this translated into $260 billion in sales and was projected to grow to $325 billion by the end of 2009. Pfizer is the world's largest firm by revenue, with 2004 sales of $52.5 billion and decreasing to an estimated $48.2 billion in 2009. In January 2009, Pfizer announced plans to acquire Wyeth, a mid-size ethical drug maker. If the deal goes through, Pfizer will have the second largest market capitalization in the industry at some $160 billion, behind Roche/ Genentech, whose combined stock value was estimated at $195 billion as of

The Varieties of Leadership at Novarum Pharmaceuticals: A Novel, pages 151–167

January 27, 2009. Revenue growth in Big Pharma is largely due to increase in the elderly population within wealthy nations.

Industry profits have been comparatively high over the past few decades, but are softening due to a variety of pressures described below and in the *Strategic threats and opportunities* table. The U.S. Bureau of Labor Statistics states that the "pharmaceutical and medical manufacturing industry" employed 293,000 people in 2004. However, many firms have cut jobs as a way to control costs. More than 100,000 jobs have been cut in the past 5 years. For instance, Merck cut 10,000 jobs since its 2005 recall of the painkiller Vioxx and plans another 7,200 job cuts by 2011 when a key patent expires. As more firms merge, job cuts are a likely result. For instance, Pfizer has stated its intention to cut thousands of jobs after acquiring Wyeth. Similarly, in March 2009, Merck announced its intention to acquire Schering Plough, and analysts expect the merged firm will reduce its payroll substantially.

The pharmaceutical industry is heavily regulated and scrutinized by several constituencies: governments, big employers, medical insurance companies, physicians, and public interest research groups [PIRGs]. Governments in nearly every nation control drug prices and manufacturing standards of quality and safety. Employers and insurance companies bargain hard for lower prices. Physicians and PIRGs advocate for more effective, easier-to-administer drugs with fewer negative side effects. In addition, investors call for short-term returns that are incompatible with the long lead-time required to create new, complex products.

Bringing a safe and effective drug to market takes 8 to 12 years and, according to some sources, costs $800 million.[2]

A successful ethical drug generally passes through several stages:

- preclinical discovery of molecules in the lab that might ameliorate or cure a specific disease;
- phase I clinical trials with healthy volunteers;
- phase II clinical trials with a small numbers of patients;
- phase III clinical trials with a large number of patients; and
- the all-important FDA approval followed by phase IV launch; that is, large-scale use and monitoring of outcomes.

Preclinical research and isolation of compounds takes about 8% of the time required to bring a new drug to market, but 30% of the cost. Because the cost of creating drugs is high, few firms have the resources—critics say ethical bearing—to invest in so-called orphan diseases with small markets.

Instead, Big Pharma concentrates their efforts on common, chronic diseases such as elevated cholesterol, high blood pressure, blood sugar imbalances, and pain medicines that require daily medications over years, not weeks.

Big Pharma is being increasingly criticized on a number of fronts. For instance, many charge that the industry squanders its resources on producing "me too" drugs that are nearly identical in performance to existing drugs such as cholesterol-reducing statins. In one recent year, the U.S. pharmaceutical industry spent $19 billion on marketing, which is much more than they spent on R&D. Novartis, for example, spent 33% of its budget on sales and marketing and only 19% on R&D. Critics maintain too much of the R&D effort is directed to relatively unimportant lifestyle "health problems," such as male-pattern baldness, wrinkled skin, or conventional shyness. Finally, industry profits are excessive—well beyond the overall S&P average. The cost of life-sustaining drugs is too high, particularly for the uninsured. A Harris poll underscores the growing unease with the industry. In 1998, consumer satisfaction stood at 50%; by 2005, consumer satisfaction had declined to a mere 15%.

The industry counters these charges by asserting they operate in a unique space: a private sector enterprise that is heavily regulated, needing to satisfy investors while not physically harming patients and pricing drugs to recoup their large R&D costs. Ethical manufacturers need to drive sales of their branded drugs fast because cheaper generics flood the market immediately after patents expire. Big Pharma notes that generic drugs account for a $70 billion share of the U.S. market alone and are projected to grow substantially as a large number of patents expire between 2010 and 2015. Advertising to patients is not bad, they argue. In fact, giving patients information about drugs allows them to play a more involved part in their own health management.

The industry also believes that, compared with the cost of hospitalization, drugs offer a much more favorable cost-benefit outcome for society. For instance, the total cost of full hip surgery can run as high as $40,000. By contrast, the cost of a year's worth of preventive medicine costs approximately $1000.

Drug Industry Quick Facts[3]

Global Industry Includes

1. Biotech firms, e.g., genetic engineering
2. Branded drug makers

3. Generic drug makers
4. Contract research organizations
5. Wholesalers
6. Retailers

Why Is th Industry Ailing?

1. R&D costs high, but yield few blockbuster drugs
2. Earnings soft by historical standards, but still yielding 20%–25% per year
3. Patents on blockbuster drugs are expiring, putting billions at risk to lower-priced generics. Four big patent-protected drugs whose patents will soon expire include Pfizer's Lipitor, Wyeth's Effexor, Merck's Singulair, and Eli Lily's Zyprexa.
4. Cheaper generic rivals are eroding sales of Big Pharma.
5. Tarnished image

Harris Poll Shows

1. 1998 = 50% consumer satisfaction
2. 2005 = 15% consumer satisfaction

Reasons Why Industry Image Is Tarnished

1. Popular anti-inflammatory drug—Vioxx (Merck)—recalled because of adverse reaction and multiple deaths
2. Exaggerated claims of industry about miracle drugs that have failed to deliver
3. "Me too" drugs heavily advertised but tackling the same problem in much the same way as existing drugs, e.g., cholesterol lowering drugs; analgesics
4. Rushing drugs to market without adequate clinical trials and withholding information on dangerous side effects
5. Pushing life-style drugs, e.g., Botox and Viagra, instead of doing research on life-threatening conditions
6. Perceived excessive profits of industry, especially relative to increasing skepticism of the drug's efficacy
7. Perceived excessive costs of drugs to patients during a worldwide recession

Six Big Constituencies and Oftentime Critics of the Industry

- Investors, especially those who want a fast ROI
- Employers who want lower drug costs for prescription plans
- Regulators
- Physicians
- Hospital administrators
- Patients

The drug industry, like others in profit-seeking health care, has a unique problem: the need to satisfy investors' desire for profit, while not alienating the general public and patients.

Some Strategic Responses of the Industry, Especially Big Pharma, to Environmental Threats and Opportunities:

1. Cut costs: e.g., (a) use seasoned sales force to answer complicated questions and use lower-skilled employees to pass out samples; and (b) streamline manufacturing operations.
2. Create specialized drugs, vaccines, instead of drugs for primary care.
3. Grow by acquiring smaller pharmaceutical and health care services firms. For instance, in January 2009, Abbott Labs agreed to buy Advanced Medical Optics, Wyeth expressed their intent to acquire Crucell, a vaccine maker, and Schering Plough acquired Organon-BioSciences. Teva Pharmaceuticals (Israeli) bought out Barr. Lily's $6.5 billion acquisition of ImClone Systems may prove costly if their products fail to deliver results.
4. Grow by acquiring large biotechnology firms, e.g., Genetech; perhaps the largest firm in its industry is likely to be acquired by Swiss drug-maker Roche Holdings in 2009.
5. Spin off operations, e.g. parts or all of manufacturing and even R&D.
6. Restructure R&D division to increase early stage clinical trials, thereby dropping ineffective drugs earlier in the testing cycle.
7. Use more powerful software to model drug behavior in a cell, tissue, or organ.
8. Use biotech engineering to create "biosimilars," the chemical equivalent of generic drugs. Biosimilars can be manufactured at a lower cost than generics.
9. Form joint ventures to attack widespread problems, e.g., diabetes, Alzheimer's, depression.

10. Conduct more intensive "Phase IV" follow-up with patients taking drugs to ensure safety and efficacy.
11. Use informatics (data mining) to more accurately and efficiently measure drug efficacy.
12. Create foundations and otherwise cut prices for drugs to the Third World. For example, Novo Nordisk (Danish) started a diabetes foundation, funded at $10m/year. Also, educate Third World citizens about lifestyle to prevent or better manage their lives in general and diseases in particular, e.g., family planning; AIDS.
13. Permit e-prescribing from manufacturers to physicians, especially in the Third World, to ensure the correct drug is given and used as intended.
14. Give incentives to physicians for achieving certain patient clinical outcomes, and therefore, lower overall costs of drugs to government, employers, and patients.
15. Bring investor expectations into line with reality by more thoroughly educating investors that it takes a long time to bring a unique drug to the market. Reduce, therefore, unrealistic expectations for fast ROI.
16. Change leadership and employee expectations regarding the more competitive nature of the industry, the need for more creative research, operational efficiency, and acceptance of reduced compensation proportionate to reduced sales and profits.
17. Collaborate with, rather than oppose, the new administration's intention to reform health care in 2009. To date, Big Pharma has opposed efforts to install price controls because the U.S. market accounts for their biggest source of profits. This opposition may soften given the severity of the global recession that began in 2008.
18. Find "biomarkers" that correlate with specific diseases to better connect patients to the correct medicine. At present, 50% of all drugs don't work for people who take them. The long-term goal is personalized medicine, based on a patient's genetic signature.

Sales Methods in Need of Change

- Drug companies are notorious for aggressive selling. Novartis spent 33% on sales and marketing in 2004 and only 19% on R&D. The U.S. industry spent $19 billion on promotion in 2004. Until very recently, the industry has responded to competition by hiring more salespeople, because of the near perfect correlation between number of sales force and sales. Firms want to drive sales of their branded drugs fast because cheaper generics flood the market immediately after their patent expires. Hence, the urgency of Big Pharma to maximize sales during their protected period. Selling drugs is particularly aggressive in the United States. Other than New Zealand, the U.S. is the only country that allows direct marketing of prescription drugs to consumers. Critics claim this is bad because patients then badger their physicians for drugs they don't fully understand. While the industry retorts that advertising empowers patients to take an active role in their own health care, more legislators are taking a dim view of that claim.

- To avoid the potential backlash from government and other stakeholders, the industry may need to soften its sales approach to physicians. Drug salespersons have relied on the three "F's"—friendship, food, and free (samples, etc.)—to gain access to physicians, but more are starting to resist the lure. Drug representatives try to convince physicians that their drug is the best treatment for diseases, but this is not necessarily the best drug for various categories of patients, or the most economical. The Obama administration is on record as having a goal to reduce drug prices.

Some Facts About the Global Market

The 2004 Pharmaceutical Market Divides as Such

- North America = 48%
- Europe = 30%
- Japan = 11%
- Latin America = 4%
- Other = 7%

Citizens in most of the developing world must pay for their own drugs; government and employers don't, and insurance is not available. Thus, the drug market is small and dominated by older generics that cost less than prescriptions. But the market is vast because of the sheer numbers—China and India's population is three times larger than the United States and European Union combined.

OXFAM criticized Big Pharma for not selling its best drugs in the Third World at a discount. Big Pharma has started discounting prices to some extent. Also, Big Pharma is increasingly concerned about public relations and is thus doing more to sell its drugs at reduced prices in poor nations.

Not only wishing to sell more drugs to the developing world, Big Pharma also wants to conduct more off-shore manufacturing because of the lower cost.

Singapore is investing billions in biomedical research. Indeed, Singapore aspires to be the center of complicated medical tourism. South Korea is making large investments into biotechnology and is expected to be a competitor of the U.S. manufacturers. Brazil intends to become a leading supplier of generics to the Third World, beginning in South America. Big Pharma may look for partnerships in these nations.

India

- India's cost for R&D is 60% lower than the United States. One reason is human resources. For instance, a highly skilled Indian chemist has a total annual compensation package of $60K, vs. $250K in the U.S.
- India allows legal protection for "process patents," i.e., how drugs are manufactured. This spawned thousands of small companies that copied branded drugs by inventing new manufacturing methods. The biggest challenge to the United States is a small Indian firm's legal challenge to Pfizer's Lipitor. Depending on outcome, the consequences will be enormous to the U.S. and Indian industry.
- India is a good place to test drugs because of its huge population and widespread fluency in English, one of its official languages. But hospitals don't have a reliable infrastructure to ensure patients adhere to protocols. Hence, Big Pharma must be extremely careful when generalizing results from Indian clinical trials.

China

- China lags behind India because of its plodding state-run industry. But it's changing fast, because China is now eagerly seeking foreign direct investment.
- The widespread practice of traditional cures, e.g., botanical sources, may give Big Pharma a place to look for molecules to isolate and test against their disease targets.
- China is far less careful about patent protection than the West, e.g., the government overturned Pfizer's patent on Viagra.

- Counterfeiting is rampant in China, even for prescription drugs. Thus, doing business in China is problematic due to the need to ensure patient safety, avoid legal liability from both legitimate and illegitimate claims, and protect the firm's public image.
- China is more aggressive than United States in some areas of biotech experimentation, i.e., using genetic engineering. Why? Less concern about patient safety, few cultural prohibitions, and a one-party state that greatly lacks checks and balances from opposition parties or a free press. This gives China, at least in the short run, a competitive advantage over Western firms. Thus, the opportunity for partnerships with Chinese firms may exist, but at present few U.S. firms are rushing in.

Notes

1. Information provided in this background concentrates on research, development, and manufacturing in the prescription drug industry, also referred to as the ethical drug makers. Many of the large firms also manufacture, distribute, and sell over-the-counter [OTC] drugs such as cough and cold preparations, vitamins, analgesics, and medicated skin products and disinfectants. The OTC market and growth rate is smaller than the prescription market, but still substantial. (See, for example, DATAMONITOR "OTC Pharmaceuticals in the United States" Ref #:0072-0364, December, 2008.)
2. The oft-cited $800 million figure comes from an industry-sponsored study at Tufts University. The actual cost is unknown, but critics charge the direct R&D cost is much less than $800 million, in part because the industry includes marketing expenses in this figure.
3. Fekl, Shereen el (2005, June 18–24) *Economist* v.375, #8431; *Value Line.* Drug Industry survey, January 16, 2009.

Pharmaceutical Industry: Strategic Threats and Opportunities

After decades of financial growth and high public regard, the industry recognizes it must adapt its approach to doing business in an increasingly competitive and skeptical environment. In general, the industry needs to (1) lower drug prices, (2) create more effective drugs for serious diseases, (3) increase the precision of drugs to address individual differences, (4) bring drugs to the market faster without compromising safety, (5) conduct methodologically rigorous Phase IV evaluations to determine patient outcomes and respond quickly and responsibly to unanticipated negative side effects, and (6) take more seriously its corporate social responsibility to put patients above profit

Strategic Opportunities Include

- Discovering the relationship between genes and specific diseases, allowing more precise prescriptions based on each patient's unique genetic makeup. (Also referred to as personalized drug therapy.)
- Outsourcing selected functions, e.g., clinical testing and chemical manufacturing, to reduce costs
- Ministering to the growing population of elderly in rich nations who require more drugs for age-related health problems, especially chronic conditions

The Varieties of Leadership at Novarum Pharmaceuticals: A Novel, pages 161–167

- Using more powerful IT software to model drug behavior in a cell, tissue, or organ, thereby collapsing the time required for research and improving understanding of molecular behavior
- Forming consortiums to address common diseases, e.g., cancers, heart disease
- Using IT data mining to better study patient outcomes and therefore refine drug properties and dosages
- Growing the over-the-counter market, especially as potent prescription drugs are made available as OTC
- Increasing revenue due to the Medicare Prescription-Drug Benefit Act (effective in 2006) that prohibits government from negotiating prices with drug manufacturers. [n.b. This Act may be modified under the Obama administration.]
- Increasing sales of nutritional supplements and vitamins
- Exploring joint ventures with more distantly related firms. For example, CVS is the largest drugstore chain in the U.S., with annual sales of $76.3 billion in 2008. CVS, through its acquisition of Caremark, is now larger than Johnson and Johnson. The chain's goal is to help transform America's expensive and inefficient prescription drug market in line with President Obama's stated goal of reducing the cost of drugs. Caremark acts as a pharmacy benefit management company, handling the prescription drug needs for big employers, distributing drugs to employees in an efficient manner, for example, by providing 90-day refills via the mail. Big Pharma may choose to acquire or create a pharmacy benefit management company as a way to guarantee a revenue stream and help to reduce the cost of its drugs.

Strategic Threats Include

- Government, insurance industry, and consumer pressure to lower prices, fueled in part by a general disenchantment of industry to deliver "miracle drugs"
- Higher patent standards, i.e., drugs may have to demonstrate real usefulness, novelty, and be nonobvious before gaining legal protection from competition;
- Patents restricted to the drug's specific, original use
- Direct-to-consumer advertising banned
- Meaningful limits placed on incentives to dispensing physicians

- Government either denies patents or requires more rigorous clinical trials for "me too" drugs that are not significantly different from existing drugs
- Consumer interest in alternative medicine, e.g., acupuncture, homeopathic, hypnosis, continues to lessen demand for conventional prescription drug therapy
- Generic drugs, and "near substitute" generics increasingly used
- Re-importation into the United States of U.S.-made drugs, but at lower prices spreads
- Industry consolidation, e.g., mergers and acquisitions, international players, causing more powerful competition to U.S. firms
- Technical challenges of creating effective drugs for more complex diseases, e.g., viruses, neurological dysfunctions.
- Slowness of Big Pharma's corporate culture—formed in a different, less competitive era—to adapt to international competition, technological advances, e.g., bioengineering and social change
- Increased FDA and Department of Justice scrutiny and patient revolt stemming from the industry's unethical and illegal practices. For instance, Pfizer was fined $2.3 billion in early 2009 for promoting its pain killer, Bextra, for nonapproved purposes. These so-called off-label promotions are illegal. Pfizer was also fined $900 million to settle lawsuits against the firm for heart attacks and strokes caused by Bextra and Celebrex, and its subsidiary Warner-Lambert incurred fines of nearly $500 million for similar off-label promotions. Eli Lily agreed to pay $1.4 billion for off-label promotions. GlaxoSmithKline had to settle claims against it for Medicare and Medicaid fraud and for withholding negative results from some of its drugs. It also had to pay the IRS $3.4 billion in a tax dispute it lost. Giants Schering Plough, Bayer, Merck, Abbott and AstraZeneca have also been fined for illegal and unethical practices. Negative publicity could spur Congress to pass legislation setting price controls on drugs, something the industry strongly opposes.

Bibliography—Corporate Fiction

Bing, S. (2003). *You look nice today.* New York: Bloomsbury.
Crichton, M. (1993). *Disclosure.* New York: Ballantine.
Heller, J. (1961). *Catch-22.* New York: Simon & Schuster.
Heller, J. (1974). *Something happened.* New York: Simon & Schuster.
Kemske, F. (1992). *Lifetime employment.* North Haven, CT: Catbird Press.
Kemske, F. (1993). *The virtual boss.* North Haven, CT: Catbird Press
Kemske, F. (1995). *Human resources: A corporate nightmare.* North Haven, CT: Catbird Press.
Kemske, F. (2000). *Labor day.* North Haven, CT: Catbird Press.
Lodge, D. (1975). *Changing places.* London: Penguin Books.
Mamet, D. (1982). *Glengarry Glen Ross: A play.* New York: Grove Press.
McInerney, J. (1984). *Bright lights, big city.* New York: Vintage
Miller, A. (1949). *Death of a salesman.* New York: Viking Press.
Mortimer, J. (1983). *The first Rumpole omnibus.* London: Penguin Books
Nothomb, A. (2002). *Fear and trembling.* New York: Faber & Faber.
Roth, P. (2000). *The human stain: A novel.* New York: Vintage International.
Russo, R. (1998). *The straight man.* New York: Vintage Contemporaries.
Wade, B. (1993). *Company man.* Chapel Hill, NC: Algonquin Books.
Weisberger, L. (2003). *The devil wears Prada.* New York: Random House.
Wilson, S. (1955). *The man in the gray flannel suit* . New York: Four Walls Eight Windows Press.
Wolfe, T. (1987). *The bonfire of the vanities: A novel.* New York: Farrar, Straus & Giroux.

The Varieties of Leadership at Novarum Pharmaceuticals: A Novel, page 165

Index

The Varieties of Leadership at Novarum Pharmaceuticals: A Novel, pages 167–170

V

W

www.ingramcontent.com/pod-product-compliance
Lightning Source LLC
LaVergne TN
LVHW052327200926
848481LV00002B/693